Y0-BDS-848

ESCAPE TO LIFE

A Journey Through the Holocaust

ESCAPE TO LIFE

A Journey Through the Holocaust

The Memories of
MARIA AND WILLIAM HERSKOVIC

PATRICIA HERSKOVIC

Yad Vashem • Jerusalem • 2002

Language Editor: Alifa Saadya

The events and conversations detailed in this book took place decades ago and were reconstructed from the memories of my parents. For this reason they are as accurate as memory allows, but are true in substance and tone.

ISBN — 965-308-152-7

Published by Yad Vashem
P.O.B. 3477, Jerusalem 91034
e-mail: publications.marketing@yadvashem.org.il

Printed in Israel 2002
by Daf Noy, Jerusalem

"Even the helpless victim of a hopeless situation, facing a fact he cannot change, may rise above himself, may grow beyond himself, and by so doing change himself. He may turn a personal tragedy into a triumph."

Viktor E. Frankl, Man's Search for Meaning

Contents

Dedication

This work is dedicated to all those who suffered from the Nazi oppression and genocide, including my aunts and uncles, and especially Germaineke and Katie, the tiny sisters I never knew who were killed in the gas chambers of Auschwitz in September of 1942.

It is also very much dedicated to all those angels who had the courage to help my parents in their odysseys for survival, including Georges De Groote, his parents, Warren, Fincha and *Bomma* Abrams, Helen Gillot, Margaretha Diedrighs, the Linchamps, Mme. Ackard, Professor Chaim Perelman of the Comité de Défense des Juifs en Belgique, and a host of others, may they be tavern owners, workmen, doctors, civil clerks or seamstresses who, when given the opportunity, chose to act with goodness despite the risk of death.

Most of all, this book is dedicated to its heroes — my heroes and parents, Maria and William Herskovic, who have consistently filled my every day with their limitless passion for life and love of family.

I would also like to give special thanks to my husband, Jack Freedman, for his extraordinary support and input; to my son, James, for his patience and creative insights; my sisters, Micheline Keller and Suzanne Ponder, for their encouragement and reminders of this project's urgency; my stepdaughters, Robyn and Jill, for always believing in my abilities, and all my friends who indulged me with open ears and thoughtful comments (Joyce and Jeannine in particular for doing so with pencils in hand). I would also like to thank Rabbi May of the Simon Wiesenthal Center for offering, and Aaron Breitbart for executing, an early historical accuracy read; and Dr. Robert Trafeli for moving more than my bones, for without him I might have only seen the darkness of the Holocaust and missed the magic of survival completely.

Last, but certainly not least, I would like to thank Dr. Bella Gutterman, Shraga Mekel, and Yad Vashem for kindly, enthusiastically, and ever so swiftly consenting to publish; and for gracing me with Alifa Saadya, who, though brought on as an editor, became much, much more. Thank you, Alifa, for helping me to complete the story of my parents' magical journey, which evolved into an incredible journey of my own.

Prologue

I always knew we were a little different. Well, maybe not always. I guess I first became conscious of it at the age of eight when, while having a friend over to play, my mother came in to discuss something with me. I don't remember the subject of the conversation, but I do remember the expression on my young friend's face. Confusion. Total confusion.

"You understood that?"

"What?"

"That. That — what your mom was saying. You understood that?"

"Well, sure," I responded with a little confusion of my own.

My friend explained that she hadn't understood a word of it. So, in a way, I guess that was the beginning. Apparently we'd always spoken three languages simultaneously in our house. And, for years I never even noticed. We'd only actually started with two, French and Yiddish. It wasn't until we moved to America, the San Fernando Valley to be exact, in the spring of '57, that English became a staple.

So, other than that, I guess we were just your average Southern Californian family. We'd get home from school to fresh bread, butter, and chocolate candy bar sandwiches. The candy was usually a slab of Hershey bar as the global economy wasn't full-tilt yet and the finer Belgian and Swiss brands hadn't thus far made it to our shores. The abundance of these chocolate sandwiches probably aided our popularity — once word got out, we became a frequent stop for many of our friends on their way home from school.

My mother went in to work with my father every day. He had a camera store in Westwood Village: Bel Air Camera. He chose the name for the adjacent, exclusive residential neighborhood that he planned on, and succeeded in, catering to. With my parents went my seventeen-year-old cousin Samy in an unofficial apprenticeship to my father. My auntie, Samy's mother, stayed behind to care for my two sisters and me, and to cook for the enormous and long extended family meal with which we ended each day.

With dinner we all drank beer. We never had a soda in the fridge, just beer. I even remember that, for a couple of years, half of the Frigidaire's bottom shelf was dominated by a large, shiny aluminum barrel that supplied beer on tap. I found the thing incredibly aesthetic. I'm sure it was probably designed by the same guy who conceptualized that stunning Airstream trailer of the same era. On the shelf above was seltzer. This was delivered regularly in postwar bottles with stainless steel spigots — well, regularly up until my girlfriend next door had one explode on her, badly cutting her leg. Everyone mumbled how fortunate she was that it wasn't worse. A statement that pretty much summed up the overall philosophy of our home....

It always "could've been a lot worse."

After all, it had been, but we'll get to that.

I remember the first car. A perfect car for an immigrant from Belgium (with one of the wettest climates next to that of Brazil's rainforest). A Chevrolet Bel Air convertible. Red, with a chrome-trimmed white stripe. The ignition key was gold with inlaid rubies. That key was the most exciting thing I'd ever seen. And frankly, the awe I'd held for it back then has probably never been exceeded.

Sundays were always special. A trip to Builder's Emporium with my father to buy some fascinating tool off the 25-cent table. The nursery for plants — fruit trees that all flourished under his expert supervision, while wild squirrels, pigeons, and blue jays ate from his hands. There wasn't any other wildlife around, or I'm sure it would've been eating out of his hands, too.

And then the beach. Sunny or not, Santa Monica called to us. My father would walk into the waves and start swimming, not to return for what seemed a lifetime. No matter how many times I saw this picture — the enormity of the ocean and sky, the image of my father moving in smoothly to tame this wild beast — I suppose I was always just a little afraid he wouldn't come back out.

All this was book-ended with alternating biannual trips to the Riviera Hotel in Vegas and the formidable Hotel Del Coronado. The trips were chronicled in a four-hour film my father created by editing the Super 8 and 16-mm footage from years of Vegas and Coronado trips. What was most entertaining in viewing his compilation was that from the look of things, nothing of substance really changed during those years. I mean, breasts got bigger, mascara got thicker, eyeliner came and went, and we ate. We ate before the pool, we ate after the pool, and we ate before the shows and during them. We snacked during excursions and always seemed to enjoy an ice cream cone whenever we found an empty moment.

I knew we were from Belgium. I knew my parents were calmer and more interested in us than any of our friends' parents seemed to be in them. I knew we were short on relatives. But that was about it until one summer day, sometime before my ninth birthday. I had walked by the dining room and noticed my mother and aunt crying. As they noticed me, they quickly threw something into the sideboard and closed the drawer tight.

Like any normal kid, I waited for them to leave and checked it out. There, next to the silverware, was something pink. I pulled out the beginnings of an extraordinarily beautiful hand-crocheted dress. The front half of a tiny and precious little thing. The detail was exquisite.

"Why would something so beautiful make anyone cry?"

I quickly and carefully put the unfinished dress back into the drawer and headed for the kitchen. Everything of any importance took place in the kitchen. Good, bad, didn't matter. It was where my mother would serenade our dishwashing with Edith Piaf renditions of *Milord*, which would eventually give me my first education on prostitution and the relationship of the good-hearted and strong hooker to the fragile male. It was where my mother explained that the prophylactics my sisters found under my parents' bed were finger protectors used for peeling potatoes. Amazing that she had no problem explaining prostitution, but wouldn't cop to her own marital sexual exploits. She actually put one of the little rubber shields onto her finger and demonstrated how protected she was while zealously peeling a potato.

The kitchen was the center of our home and it was there that I confronted my mother and aunt as they prepared dinner. I questioned them about the little pink dress and their tears, and I was given the beginning of a seemingly endless story that would fill my every pore for the rest of my life.

The Holocaust.

Our Holocaust.

How four short years could have been packed with so many events boggles the mind. I mean, I've lived entire years I can't remember.

I knew there had been a war in Europe. I knew my parents had suffered. I knew I'd lost family. But I suppose I never really knew how close to me that family had been. I'd had two more sisters. Two more sisters that I never knew. Two sisters that had been murdered in the gas chambers of Auschwitz years before my birth. One four-year-old, and one fourteen-month-old who was tiny enough to fit into that unfinished dress her mother had been crocheting for her to wear on her escape voyage across the ocean.

Esther, the girls' mother and my father's first wife, was also my mother's sister. She, along with her children, had been killed by the Nazis, and her absence was always a profound presence in our home.

As I grew, so did my curiosity and my father's desire to tell bedtime stories. Not the fluffy ones most children hear, but the ones that explained why I never knew Esther... or Izi, or Katie, or Linka, or Miksha, or any one of the unfamiliar faces I'd find in old photo albums. My father's tales were filled with tears and a strength beyond comprehension. My mother's, on the other hand, were filled with suppressed pain and a humor that protected her, and, for that matter, all of our psyches. Some children of survivors grew up feeling their parents were victims — weak and broken. Not me. My parents were heroes. Survivors beyond all odds, and more importantly, heroes by every definition of the word.

Chapter One

The Station

Brussels, Belgium, 1945

Why is it when we race through a crowd we hear only our footsteps? Frantic. Clicking. The only thing that will possibly drown them out is the sound of our own heartbeat as it pounds in our ears. My father seemed as anxious as my mother to get to the train. When they finally arrived and he helped her on, he didn't say good-bye.

"If you get to Theresienstadt, and Izi is dead, I want you to marry me."

Not your usual proposal. Not your usual romance.

My mother, Mireille (or *Mirele*, pronounced Mirella), still a mere twenty-one years of age, was both sensuous and savvy. She'd walked through the perils of war with a self-confidence one can only be born with. She'd seen and experienced things that destroy souls, but hers survived through an incredible ability to laugh, finding humor even in the most difficult of times. Finding ironies and adventures at every turn. The years that many of us spent learning about the world in universities' hallowed halls, she spent in attics and hidden apartments where she learned of human nature's extremes.

She stared at my father, William, with amazement as the train left the station. Her surprising suitor was a lanky young man of thirty, known as Willy. His dark hair and a pencil-thin mustache reinforced his strong linear features and angular face, whose dark young eyes spoke of anything but youth, for youth is innocence, and captured in war, innocence is never taken prisoner, but always killed. And in Willy's case, its death occurred only after long and painful torture.

He stood on the platform of the train station and watched as the smoke obscured his vision of Mirele's surprised face. He stood there till the train traveled so far that it was nowhere to be seen. He stood there till his mind traveled even further. Back. Back to the beginning of the war.

Chapter Two

First Warning — Willy

> "He is the God of the unexpected, of luck, of coincidences, of synchronicity. 'Hermes has entered our midst,' the ancient Greeks would say when a sudden silence entered the room, descended on conversation, and introduced into the gathering another dimension. Whenever things seem fixed, rigid, stuck, Hermes introduces fluidity, motion, new beginnings — and the confusion that almost inevitably precedes new beginnings."
>
> Arianna Huffington, *The Gods of Greece*

Fate.

Destiny.

Luck.

People have argued as to their existence for centuries, and will continue to do so until the end of time, with a resolution to the debate unlikely at best.

Mazel, the Yiddish word for "luck," on the other hand, has a far more interesting definition than its English counterpart. *Mazel* is more specifically defined as "being in the right place, at the right time, and having the knowledge that you're there." With *mazel* then, we accept the notion that luck may exist, but its worth is only actualized through the recipient's active participation.

At fifteen, my father was working as an apprentice photographer in Czechoslovakia (it was still part of Hungary the year he was born, and Slovakia today). Each Friday he would board the same six o'clock bus that would take him from town to the village of his grandparents' farm, where he spent every weekend. Each Friday at six o'clock, until one particular Friday. That day, he boarded as usual but happened to catch his reflection in the side mirror. He was stunned to see the whites of both his eyes a terrifying solid pitch black. Instantly, he jumped down off the steps and went directly to the local doctor.

"I've never seen or heard of anything like this," the doctor told the frightened boy as he studied his eyes.

He went to a glass cabinet and pulled out a small bottle.

"Put a few drops of this into your eyes twice a day," he looked at the concerned youth for a beat and continued, "Take the next bus home. Relax with your grandparents for the weekend, and I will research. You come back to see me Monday. I will have some information for you."

Willy did as the doctor instructed and boarded the next bus to the country, and when he finally entered the farmhouse, was shocked to see his grandmother crying inconsolably.

"*Grossmutter*, what is it?" he questioned her.

She tried to calm her tears. "You're alive," she said with quiet astonishment, throwing her arms around her adored grandchild.

She explained in lurid detail that the six o'clock Friday bus he'd always taken had collided with an oncoming train. Two passengers, who stood holding the ceiling straps, flew away from the site along with the roof of the vehicle. They survived. Everyone else on the crowded bus had died.

"*Dein Vater* is there now... looking for your body," she began to weep all over again. "Thank God you're safe."

With these words, Willy suddenly realized his grandmother hadn't mentioned the strange blackness of his eyes. He quickly went to a nearby mirror and found they were one hundred percent back to normal.

Everyone marveled at his luck. The romantic might believe he
had an angel. His mother perhaps, having died when he was just
six months old, had been unable to abandon her infant son and
continued to watch over him throughout his life. This would
possibly explain all the future "luck" that would befall him in the
years that followed. As with the tragedy of the bus, sometimes
extreme luck is only apparent in the most difficult situations —
situations that would themselves seem most unlucky. So, in
examining the extraordinarily frequent appearance of profound
luck in my father's life, one could say he suffered the worst luck
imaginable, or the best.

Willy was twenty-four when the horrors of World War II began
to engulf him. Seven years earlier he'd left his home in
Czechoslovakia to join his family in Antwerp. Prior to that, at a
mere thirteen years of age, Willy had decided to fulfill the
commitment he'd made as an apprentice photographer,
remaining behind when his father, stepmother, and younger
siblings had fled their home in search of a freedom they weren't
afforded in the East. In the four short years of his photographic
apprenticeship in Eastern Europe, my father had acquired skills
great enough to find an almost immediate success in this
prospering Jewish community. Even today, any prewar
Antwerp Jew whom I come across remembers or cherishes one
of his photographs.

As the years went by, it seemed that there wasn't a wedding or
Bar Mitzvah portrait that he didn't shoot. Every new romance
or baby sat before his camera for documentation. His artistic
abilities were lauded, and his female subjects were certain they
would never look more beautiful than on the day they posed
before his camera. He looked upon every photograph as a work
of art, even if it meant restyling his subject's hair. Rather deft

with the curling iron, his "casualties" were few. On the rare occasion that hair seared and dropped to the floor, he would quickly begin to light his subject. With just the slightest adjustment of a lamp or reflector, he made the heavy appear svelte, and the thin, voluptuous. His retouching pencil was good enough to correct any of nature's imperfections, and somehow the slight damage he might have caused to any young woman's hair was always forgotten by the time she was handed her portrait.

By 1936, at the age of 22, he had married. His wife, Esther, was a natural Claudette Colbert. Statuesque in homemade dresses fastidiously fashioned from the photos in Hollywood movie magazines, nineteen-year-old Esther was the most exquisite creature he'd ever seen. And she adored him. Sixty-four years later, a tiny portrait of her, with a smile that caused her nose to wrinkle and her almond-shaped eyes to glow, still has a place in my father's wallet. A year after they wed, though Esther and Willy were no more than children themselves, their first daughter, Katie, was born.

Katie filled my father's heart in ways he'd never thought possible. She would stand beside him every available minute of every day, her arms wrapped around one of his legs whether he was shooting pictures or working in the darkroom.

So, by twenty-five years of age, he found himself surrounded by friends, family, and a quiet success. Life was as close to perfection as he could have imagined. A dream. But the sad truth about perfect dreams is that one is forced to wake to a reality that can never quite measure up. Or even worse, dreams sometimes turn to nightmares. And the price of William's dream was that he was forced to suffer a melding of the two. With the onslaught of World War II, my father was to wake to a reality that was to become a living nightmare.

22

You could say his suffering started slowly. Maybe it was in early 1939 when he began to receive postcards from a concentration camp in Poland. The letters came from his older sisters, Ethel and Rosie (*Roshie*), still living in Czechoslovakia. The Germans had taken all the Jews from his hometown in Fishar. He was directly related to thirty-two of them.

Siblings.

Cousins.

And if there can be a quantification of this type of loss, the gravest was probably that of his grandparents — the tender loving farmers who had reared him from infancy after the untimely death of his mother. Recently, he found painful solace in learning that his grandmother died en route to the camps. For fifty years he'd imagined her suffering at the hands of the German guards. At least now he learned it hadn't been for too long.

Willy and Esther sent packages to Ethel and Rosie when those first letters came. Then a month later, though there was no response, they sent packages again, and then, once again — but they never received another letter. And in fact, not one of his thirty-two Czech family members was ever seen again.

My father's Antwerp storefront, with its large meticulously painted sign that read "STUDIO WILLY," stood not far from a refugee way-station of sorts. Many of those fleeing the Nazis in Germany would travel to Belgium where they were given transit papers to their desired destinations. And for these papers, the refugees needed photos.

These sudden nomads flocked to his studio day after day, water often oozing from their shoes, still wet from illegally crossing borders. Usually unable to escape Germany with cash, many brought with them the popular Leica 3A camera. They'd come to Willy wanting to sell, but the conversation always turned to war. The first wave of refugees warned him of the problems in Germany. But soon the warnings included Austria, and later, Czechoslovakia. They warned that Belgium was not nearly far enough from the Nazis' reach.

"Canada, America, Africa. You must leave immediately... Hitler will be here too," one customer, whose wet shoes had left patterns on the studio's clean floor, cautioned him excitedly.

Their faces changed, but the words were always the same. Willy so wanted to heed their warnings, but Esther was not ready to leave her family, and for the most part, life in Antwerp was still oddly unchanged. But not for long.

In September 1939, Poland was invaded. Two days later, England and France declared war. They put more men on the fronts and guarded borders, but there was no offensive action.

The BBC announced, "Quiet on the front, no fighting in the West... Poland is finished." Everyone in local taverns speculated as to what this meant.

In less than a month, eastern Poland was acquired by Russia, and western Poland by Germany. The country was totally closed off after being occupied, and the Nazis did their best to keep the situation there a mystery to the rest of the world. To outsiders like Willy, this was only a military situation and not at all about Polish civilians. But the horrifying shrouded reality was that Hitler's soldiers had already killed thousands of

doctors,

priests,

students,

Communists and artists.

Mothers.

Fathers.

Children.

And on May 10th, 1940, Germany invaded France, Holland, Luxembourg, and Belgium.

My father lay beside his young wife in deep sleep. The sounds of shooting caused her to stir and awaken him. He quickly pulled on his clothes and shoes and went out onto the street where he heard the anti-aircraft cannons that were Belgium's defense. The days of burying their heads in the sands of optimism were over. War was undeniably on their doorstep.

By morning, throngs of people moved through the streets with a turbulent uncertainty that was now to become a way of life. Esther and Willy found their way through the dazed hysteria to the British Consulate. Though she was the child of two Russian immigrants, Esther had been born in a refugee camp in England during World War I, giving her British citizenship, good for an immediate passage to the U.K. Facing lines, desks, and bureaucrats at every turn, she and Willy found themselves telling one after another of her British citizenship. The Consul prepared a passport for Esther and Katie on the spot, and told them to go to the coast as soon as possible. He explained that for the moment the English military was picking up all English citizens, but that there was no way of knowing how long this would be feasible.

Esther and Willy prepared for the trip along with an English friend, Fanny Hasser, and her own young husband. In addition to baby Katie, Willy's young teenage brother, Armand, joined them. Driven by Fanny's brothers, they traveled by truck toward the coast some fifty kilometers away. Whenever my father looks back at these early war days he remains haunted by a painful reality that he's never really been able to reconcile — the concept that the thing we've called luck had decided never to rear its head for his wife and child, for at every single turn, whenever the fire of hope flared, it was quickly extinguished.

This particular time, halfway through their journey to the coast, in the darkest of the night, they were stopped by local authorities. Though raising the children in the Czech countryside, Willy's stepmother was Viennese and had hired a German tutor to instruct them. As a result, German was their strongest language. The French authorities quickly realized the young travelers spoke German as well as Flemish, and since war breeds fear, and fear spawns paranoia, they were suspected of being spies. They were all imprisoned and interrogated, and although set free by morning, had lost a day of travel.

The Germans, meanwhile, were quickly moving into Belgium. As this small band of travelers approached the border that would lead to the coast and the English ships that offered freedom, Esther began to panic. She feared Willy's Czech papers would prevent his passage, and she refused to leave him. The tragic irony remains, that if they'd only known the outcome of the war and of my father's incredible tale of survival, how different things might have been that day....

My father and his young family spent three days at the French border town of Lapanne, arguing about their immediate future. Eventually, Esther's passion, and the stubbornness it fueled, prevented her from boarding the ship that sailed her friend Fanny and her husband to survival. The luck was there. The *mazel* was not.

Esther finally agreed to attempt to board the next ship, but only if they were joined by her youngest sister, Mirele, and their parents (my mother and grandparents). So, to that end, Willy hired Fanny's brothers to go back and pick them up.

Chapter Three

The Road to Lapanne — Mirele

Brussels Train Station, 1945

"If you get to Theresienstadt, and Izi is dead, I want you to marry me."

My mother, Mirele, stared back in quiet confusion as the train pulled out of the station. She didn't take her eyes off Willy till there was no more of him to see.... And then, the one she did see was someone hiding in the shadows of her mind.

Antwerp, 1923

On July 27th, Mirele made her rather dramatic entrance into the world. After hours of labor my grandmother, Souria Maschkivitzan, was about to give birth to the fifth of her children when the doctor announced that the infant was upside-down. With much effort, he finally delivered a rather "blue" baby, and immediately realized that both the newborn and the mother were near death.

"I can only save one," he announced as a question.

Somehow the decision was made that the mother of four would be the priority, and he literally tossed Mirele to the floor beneath while performing his medical miracles on Souria. Fortunately, my grandmother's sister, who was assisting in the delivery, grabbed my mother and tossed her from hot to cold water, performing whatever loving and instinctual miracles she could on her tiny niece. It might have been right then and there,

27

just a few moments into the world, that my mother learned that existence required work, and that living and survival were to be synonymous in her lifetime.

Growing up, Mirele loved her family enormously, and though they were far from well off, she lived a rather normal and fun-filled adolescence. During her school years, she'd balanced her time between studies, crushes (of which there were many), American films, and the JASC — *Joodsche Arbeiders Sport Club* (Jewish Workers Sport Club) — a lengthy name for a bunch of blue-collar kids who wanted to share a good time.

The JASC was probably the most predictable part of her life. On Mondays, they met for ice cream; Tuesdays, they did athletics in a rented gym; Wednesdays, they swam together in an indoor pool; Thursdays, they met to discuss their meetings; Fridays, they assembled to attend the newest Hollywood film; and Saturdays and Sundays were for dancing. During the Thursday meeting they would all pool their pennies and turn them over to one of their most trusted members, Leon Helfgott. Sometime before the weekend, Leon would take the precious cash to the record store where he would purchase that week's latest American release to be added to their collection.

Deported soon after the onset of the war, Leon would eventually die in the camps. His brother Simon, another member of the youth group, would survive the war years only to be killed in his efforts as a resistance fighter defending Belgium's liberation.

Young Mirele lived with her family in the rooms they occupied above her mother's neighborhood café. The building was large, albeit modest. It was located where Van Immerseel Straat dead-ended onto Kievits Straat. This junction was in the heart of the Jewish neighborhood — what could be called a ghetto, though no one thought of it as that until the war years. Forming a large structural "U" around the family home was the Beukelaar Chocolate Factory, the significance of which would later become extraordinary.

Mirele and her two older sisters, Esther and Regina (Riva), shared one large second-story room, whose window looked right down Van Immerseel Straat. Her parents occupied a second room, with a third reserved for her brothers. My grandmother turned the remainder of the building into a boarding house with the balance of the rooms rented to locals, as well as immigrants just passing through. A rather full-service establishment, those traveling from Eastern Europe to the Americas often benefited from her assistance in delousing before their otherwise certain rejection at ship embarkation.

This boarding house had been set up to further her entrepreneurial aspirations, as Souria had already succeeded in renting another building nearby, which she had turned into a hotel of sorts. The manor-like structure, whose entrance stairs were framed by two beautiful brass handrails, had an even more colorful clientele — gypsies. My mother was fascinated with these larger-than-life characters, and her janitorial responsibilities, which included regularly scrubbing the building's stairs, enabled her to get to know them firsthand. One of her favorite stories tells of the death of the King of the Gypsies, and the flamboyant mourning that ensued. Whether he actually died in the building or not isn't certain, but the mourners' celebration was one that rocked the neighborhood. For thirty days straight, the building was filled with drink, food, music and unparalleled gypsy-style mourning merriment, a strong contrast to pain and ritual for loss within her own community.

In addition to her innate business skills, my grandmother was an extraordinary chef. So good, in fact, that during her World

War I flight from Belgium to England, still a very young woman, she was made head cook of the refugee camp that housed her and her three children. The quality of her cooking is probably best understood through a story about a visit from the camp's primary underwriter, Baron Rothschild. Upon arriving at the camp, the Baron purportedly requested to "eat with his people," and a dinner plate, overflowing with savory delights, was put before him.

"No, you've misunderstood," he protested. "I want to eat what 'my people' are eating," the Baron continued, refusing the dish.

"But, Baron, this is exactly what your people are eating this evening."

"On what I'm giving you?" he questioned in shock, and then demanded, "I must meet the chef capable of this magic."

And with those words, the Baron was led to the kitchen to meet my grandmother, Souria.

"The Baron von Rothschild" — a voice of authority announced his entry.

The Baron approached Souria, where she was working by the stove.

"I must kiss the hand of the chef who is feeding my people so well," he said with a flourish as he took my apronned grandmother's hand and did just that.

The story ended with him handing her a rather large financial stipend of one hundred pounds (approximately $2,000 at today's rate), which she humbly pocketed while trying to feebly fix a lock of her hair into a comb.

Back in Antwerp almost twenty years later, and now the proprietress of two boarding houses, Souria fed much of the community from her own simple eatery. In happier times, the place was packed with contented consumers and gossip. It was a time when a *shtetl* custom surfaced, even in this urban environment, of providing every patron with two names — that which he had been given by his parents, and that which he'd been given by his neighbors. There was the *Roiter* (red), so called for his flaming red hair; the *Grubber* (fatso); *Krimmer kop* (crooked head), because of a vertebral birth defect that made it impossible for him to straighten his neck; the *Hoiker* (hunchback), due to an obvious curvature of the spine, and so on. Sometimes kind, sometimes not ... but always descriptive.

The *Luxembourger*, logically named for his recent immigration from nearby Luxembourg, came into the café one day and ordered his dinner from my aunt Riva.

"I'm not very hungry today," he said. "Just a half portion of *lokshen kugel* (noodle pudding)."

Never having dealt with such a request, the young woman excused herself and went to consult with her mother who was slaving in the kitchen.

"Mama, the *Luxembourger* says he isn't hungry today... he only wants a half portion."

"For how little we charge... tell him there are no half portions," my grandmother responded with no room for argument.

When Riva delivered this information, the *Luxembourger* didn't even pause, "Well, then I'll have a regular kugel... but make it a *really* big one."

Days in the café were long. Most of the clientele paid their five francs at the beginning of the day, and for that amount would be blessed for hours with my grandmother's cooking. Something light, like chopped liver or fried eggs and onions with a large loaf of bread, would be served around noon. At four, perhaps a fresh chicken soup... and in the evening, possibly a Hungarian stew. Between courses, the patrons would sometimes leave to pursue their livelihoods, returning at the appropriate hour for the next seating. But sometimes, they'd remain and amuse themselves all day long. This had been a time when laughter reigned, as my grandmother would take off her apron, hang it on a hook, and play someone a game of billiards. Naturally, there was always a bet, and thankfully, Souria always seemed to win.

Gambling was definitely in the family's blood. To my mother's oldest brother, Benny, it was more than an addiction. It was a lifestyle and a profession, with luck, more often than not, on his side. And when he hit big, his colossal generosity made everyone a winner. One sunny afternoon when my mother was twelve years old, he drove into town in a brand new shiny Duesenberg. He stood beside the automobile honking till she and her friends came running onto the street to see him. To young Mirele's delight, the entire back seat was jammed full of beautiful display dolls, each a collector's item with an intricately hand-painted porcelain face and outfitted in a stunning silk costume. Few girls in the neighborhood owned even one doll, and suddenly Mirele had a room filled with them. How could she not adore this bigger-than-life character, right out of a Fitzgerald novel, nattily dressed in three-piece white suits with perfectly shaped Borsolinos, or Italian sweaters with English driving caps?

I well understood her feelings, as during my own adolescence we would drive up to our home in Los Angeles to find shipments of antiques and jewelry sitting outside our front door. Thousands of dollars' worth of goods just sitting there waiting for us, the trappings of one of Benny's poker table scores. A beautiful diamond ring for one of my sisters; a delicate emerald one for me. But no matter the depth of his commitment to the game, he was smart enough to know that although one night might bring a fortune, the next might bring disaster. He possibly thought of his younger sister as better than a bank, for usually just weeks after the arrival of such a wealth of gifts, my mom would receive the call.

"Mirele, can you help me out of a jam," Benny would ask. "I'm a little low on cash for the moment... fact is, I'm broke."

The sum of the "some cash" was usually close to the cost of the gifts earlier bestowed, so my mom always felt she was coming out even.

My grandfather also had the gambling bent. So much so, that he often forgot he had five children to support and care for. He left that responsibility to his wife, who worked tirelessly to accomplish it. Late into the evenings, when she'd stopped serving food, her tables would be lent to the community for the locals' amusement. A backroom poker parlor of sorts. As the men played on, she would sit into the wee hours beside a table, usually falling asleep, her head propped up on one arm. In the mornings when she awoke to an empty room, she would reach into the deep pockets of her apron and always find a handful of francs left by the generous winners of the night before.

Mirele's early days were filled with school, an active social life, and the scrubbing of stairs in their two boarding houses. She often helped her mother throughout the afternoon however she could, but the evenings of her adolescent years were spent with the youth group or at spontaneous casual gatherings that sprang up at friends' homes throughout the neighborhood. When the Jewish curfew was eventually enforced by the Nazis, the teen satiated her need to socialize by sitting in her second-floor window. There, she could see and talk with many of her friends who were perched in similar windows across the street and even down on Van Immerseel Straat. And there, they continued to grow up, chatting through the night about crushes, and homework, and crushes. Probably in that order.

By the time 1939 rolled around, Mirele had completed her schooling. She was now sixteen and decided to find work in the world of hair styling. A romantic choice probably influenced by the dramatic ways of the Hollywood movies she so loved. As was her way, she picked the most élite salon she'd heard about, located on nearby Pelican Straat, and secured a position as stylist's assistant — best described as the girl who handed the stylist the rollers and pins, and, of course, took care of the hair washing that proceeded any "do." Her wit and cheerful demeanor cemented quick friendships with her co-workers, and though work took the bulk of her time, her social life continued to flourish.

But as with Willy and Esther, the warning signals of the war were coming in loud and clear. The chaos that had hit the streets definitely helped in making a quick decision when Fanny's brothers appeared.

"We've left Willy and Esther at the border; they're waiting for you there," the boys explained. "Esther has refused to leave until you arrive. You must collect your things immediately. There isn't a moment to spare."

By this time, my grandmother had tired of the restaurant business, and the tables had been replaced by a used clothing store that my grandfather ran. But regardless of the inventory he'd managed to amass, there was little thought before locking the door and boarding the truck. So, within minutes, Mirele and her parents were on the road.

In the midst of complete turmoil, they made their way to Lapanne. The sights along the road out of Belgium might have surprised anyone, but for a girl of sixteen, they were mind-boggling. People by the hundreds walked with children and suitcases and the odd piece of furniture. Objects more precious than anything my mother or her family had ever owned, lay abandoned in the dirt. Before beginning their trek by foot, people had grabbed what had been their most cherished possessions just hours before. But these sterling silver candelabras and platters soon became nothing more than heavy burdens, and were simply discarded like yesterday's garbage.

Willy and Esther had spent the nights waiting at a grange (pasture) along with hundreds, perhaps thousands, of others. They'd all created a spontaneous refugee camp of sorts. It was there, amidst the unfathomable chaos, that Fanny's brothers dropped off my mother and grandparents, and that they heard a call from the crowd.

"Mama," a voice called out from somewhere in the sea of people. "Mama."

Now "Mama" might have caught the attention of half of any crowd, but the voice was immediately recognized by my grandmother. Souria turned toward it and was quickly embraced by her most flamboyant child. Benny had been living the high life in Paris at the time, but when he heard of the turmoil that had enveloped his mother, he'd made a beeline for Antwerp. Once there, he was told that his family had left for the border. And though it was far from clear how he'd found them amidst this swarm of refugees, no one was surprised, as his love for, and dedication to, his mother was well known.

Mirele had always adored her brother's penchant for meticulous dress, so she was shocked to see him in his present condition. The suit was still white as usual, but this time, wrinkled and dirty. He still wore a tie, despite the fact that he seemed to have lost the collar to his custom-made shirt along the way. And like a vagabond, he carried an almost comical bag at the end of a stick. But despite all the physical irregularities, he still brought his usual spark.

Chapter Four

Evil Unmasks — Willy

While awaiting the arrival of her family, Willy incessantly begged Esther to cross into France and wait on the other side of the border, but she refused. Though only a day passed before the arrival of her family, the border to France was now closed to civilians to allow the French army passage into Belgium. When it was finally reopened three days later, my grandfather, a turn-of-the-century immigrant, was stopped because of his Russian passport. But Benny, also without proper papers, just seemed to find a way through — bringing his parents and sister right along with him.

Unfortunately, as chaotic as the previous journey had been, it had now become treacherous. German planes flew overhead, dropping bombs as the Belgian refugees began to walk toward their uncertain destinations. German rapid-fire machine guns sprayed the roads covered with people. Constantly having to dive to the safety of roadside trenches, my father covered Katie's tiny body with his own to protect her from the shrapnel that fell everywhere around them.

Their journey continued like this for two days. The German army moved faster and deeper into France. Although Germany was in the process of achieving goals that had little to do with this handful of civilian refugees, they were trapped in the process all the same.

When travel became unbearable, they found a farm that had obviously been abandoned and decided they had no choice but to remain there in a stranger's home — Esther, baby Katie, Willy, his fifteen-year-old brother Armand, my grandparents, Mirele, and her two older brothers. Within a couple of days, as political conditions worsened, the farmer — who had also attempted to flee, returned on foot with his family, suitcases in hand.

First apologizing for the intrusion, my father asked permission to stay, and as the farmer understood their plight all too well, it was granted. The extended family remained for two weeks, by which time Germany succeeded in taking Paris. With this accomplishment, German military trucks were traveling everywhere freely, and there now seemed no choice for the refugees but to look for a safe ride back to Antwerp.

Once home, life continued almost as it had always been, but for the annoying addition of Germans constantly marching about proudly. Still acting human, albeit appropriately victorious, their masks of deception continued to conceal the Third Reich's monstrous intentions. My father reopened the studio as if he'd never left. But his camera's lens, which had once focused on young brides and, later, refugees, was now dominated by soldiers who desired souvenir portraits.

Fearing they would never make it to unoccupied France as a group, my father decided it would be best to send his young brother by train to meet their parents. Young Armand did not look especially Jewish, and in addition, Willy felt that a young boy traveling alone would most probably be overlooked.

"If anyone asks for your papers, tell them your parents have them," Willy instructed as he put him on the train. "Don't be afraid. Read your book. You'll be there before you know it." Armand had a love of reading that Willy hoped would serve to distract him throughout the journey.

Meanwhile, freedoms in Antwerp were slowly chipped away.

Because it was a port town, many locals owned boats for commerce or pleasure. All of these were requisitioned by the German military and adapted to eventually cross the channel to England. Whether flat-bottomed or propeller, the Germans readied each to serve their purpose — eventually revealed in the fall of 1940.

Living amidst war, civilians became acutely aware of politics and strategy. Every meal eaten with family or friends was accompanied by conversations that dealt with nothing but news and speculation. Any victory the Allies tasted was relished. One of the greatest such victories would become known as the "Battle of Britain." Germany attacked England from the air with a seemingly never-ending stream of aircraft, intended to weaken the country in preparation for a greater invasion by water that was to follow. But for the first time since the war had begun, Germany found a formidable foe.

The German *Luftwaffe* (Air Force) was required to return to Belgium and France to refuel and reload. England had the enormous advantage of being able to quickly land to do the same, and therefore made a remarkable counterattack.

Goering had been certain he would be "King of the Air," but England felt this battle might be her only chance, and fought him wholeheartedly. So, even with the disadvantage of far fewer planes, England prevailed. Germany lost the Battle of Britain, their planes destroyed four to one — hundreds daily — for four weeks.

Losing this battle forced the Germans to rethink their strategy, so they pulled back and turned to the Balkans and Eastern Europe. There was elation at Germany's first great defeat. Everyone had broadly accepted the fact that the *Luftwaffe* was Germany's strongest tool, but now it was a little less ominous, and hope regained a footing.

The local German soldiers somehow continued to allay everyone's well-founded fears with a guise of cordiality, and for a time, Belgian refugees who had fled to the south of France began to return. This halted suddenly when France's General Pétain made a pact with Germany to detain the Jews and communists in southern refugee camps.

These refugees became a huge asset to the French, who began to exchange their new Jewish and communist prisoners for French POWs captured by the Germans. Thus, Jews and communists quickly became prisoners of the German army in Drancy, a *sammellager* (assembly camp) and detention camp in occupied France just outside Paris.

Though Hitler had been defeated in the aerial Battle of Britain, with renewed strength on land, he found success in the first part of 1941 with the taking of Yugoslavia, Albania, and Greece. Additionally, except for part of Yugoslavia, the Balkans were completely occupied by the Germans.

My father's work in his studio continued throughout this period, with only fragmented news about the war making it to Antwerp. That is, until one day in the middle of 1941, when a warning angel took the most unlikely form, perhaps that of the devil himself.

A *Hollander* (Dutchman) in a German uniform needed passport photos. Drunk and alone, he stumbled into "Studio Willy." Taking advantage of his inebriated state, my father began to solicit as much information as he could. And the more he heard, the more his head spun.

The *Hollander* explained that he was in Antwerp to set up a new *sammellager* on the outskirts of the city, and to arrange train transportation for thousands of Belgian Jews to Auschwitz in Poland.

"Camps for Jews," he proudly explained.

He sat down on the stool facing the camera, and as Willy began to set his lights, the man continued.

"We gather them here, and then send them by train. Jews, the old, and children, will eventually be gassed and burned. The rich and poor who cannot do manual labor will be killed as well."

Matter of fact: an efficient Nazi plan devoid of any human emotion.

"Is this good? How do I look?" He posed for his portrait as Willy approached the camera.

The inhumanity of his slurred statements were totally surreal to the young photographer as he performed his tasks. The *Hollander* spoke of people as perhaps only the coldest rancher might speak of his cattle, yet even the average rancher has respect for his herd, and a rational purpose for their slaughter.

Willy's worst fears were now validated, and he went numb. All his dreams of getting his beloved wife and child out of the country disintegrated before him in the form of the drunken soldier. Or was he the final warning? Was this the last chance?

From that very moment life began to change drastically. The Jews were given a seven o'clock curfew, and arrested if they disobeyed it. People once more began to flee. There was an atmosphere of chaos and desperation.

Willy photographed one Jewish immigrant who pleaded, "Right away! I'll pay you all you want for them, right away."

He told my father that there was a bureau in which German officers gave out transport papers that allowed Belgians to flee to southern France, where Willy's own parents had been for some time. As soon as he'd handed the man his photos, Willy went directly to the bureau and requested exit visas.

"Pictures?" The German officer demanded ironically. "Passport? Come back tomorrow with them and you'll have your papers."

Willy and Esther left the bureau and went directly to her parents' apartment. Esther's mother, Souria, became hysterical at the prospect of their leaving, and her hysteria changed Esther's mind. Frustrated, and completely against his instincts, Willy had no choice but to decline to pick up the papers that were promised for the following day.

The cloud of Nazi deceit began to lift even further as the financially powerful Diamond Exchange was taken over by the Germans. The diamond merchants' assets were confiscated without warning or explanation. The German presence was no longer simply a military occupation, but an immediate threat to every civilian. What the Western Europeans still didn't know was that, following Hitler's invasion of Russia on June 22, special murder squads, the Einsatzgruppen, began to massacre Jews in the villages and towns occupied by the German army.

In July 1941, Esther gave birth to their second daughter, Germaine, an extraordinarily gentle spirit who seemed never to cry. And though it was a frightening time to have a child, a time of great uncertainty, somehow as always with birth, came hope for the future, no matter how ill-founded and foolishly optimistic it may have been.

Not long afterwards, my father was working in his studio when two German soldiers came in.

"Jewish store?!" they asked.

Willy nodded cautiously.

"Why doesn't it say Jewish business?! All Jewish stores must hang a sign on the door. Why not yours?"

"I was never told to," he answered calmly.

"We're telling you now. It must say so by next week!"

Maybe it was ego or simply the folly of youth, or perhaps the independence that comes from raising oneself from childhood, but my father decided not to post the sign. The following week, a high-ranking German naval officer who had posed for his portrait the previous week was waiting for his photographs when the two young soldiers returned. Willy went to the front of the studio prepared for a confrontation.

"Where is the sign?" they demanded. "We told you all businesses must post a sign!"

"This is not a place of commerce," he explained. "I'm only an artist."

The answer did not satisfy the young soldiers, and they began to scream threats and an argument ensued. Suddenly from the back, the officer came out. The two lower-ranked soldiers saluted.

"Don't you hear? He's an artist and doesn't know anything from business and politics," he barked.

The three military men all glared at one another insanely as if they were about to pull their weapons and shoot each other. Willy was certain that they would, and that he might actually be killed in the crossfire. But the officer held his rank.

"Haven't you imbeciles anything better to do than bother an artist? Don't you realize there's a war going on?! Now, get out. Fast. And don't ever return!"

The men left with tails between their legs and Willy quickly regained his composure.

"Your photos will be just a moment," he said, disappearing into his darkroom for an instant before returning with the portraits that he handed to the officer.

"Thank you," the man said.

"Thank you," Willy responded.

The officer left the studio, and surprisingly, Willy never heard from any of them again.

The months of uncertainty crept by. Willy and Esther found their greatest outside support in a gentile friend named Georges

De Groote. His father had worked for my father retouching photographs in simpler times. Now, with each evening's seven o'clock Jewish curfew, came Georges. The time he spent with them helped the hours to pass, but more so, revealed his solidarity and friendship. Small acts such as a simple visit meant a lot in times of war.

More news arrived daily, along with greater numbers of German-Jewish refugees. And as before, though specifics differed, their story was always the same:

"Businesses are all closed, and we are only allowed to shop from noon to one."

"Our children are no longer allowed to attend school."

"Those who were once friends treat us as strangers."

"What strangers? Much worse, they treat us as enemies."

The option of seeking refuge in unoccupied France had disappeared. Given France's trading of Jews, the Nazi threat was now in full tilt, and everyone feared for their lives. Though young Armand had safely rejoined his parents, he left them once again to smuggle himself into Spain with a group of teens. They walked for miles through the mountains that separated the countries, only to be arrested on the other side. He was eventually released from the Spanish prison on his promise to board a boat bound for Palestine. Given a permit as part of a British quota, he embarked in Cadiz and traveled with hundreds like him on the Nyassa to Palestine. After a short stay at a kibbutz, he joined the Palestine Regiment of the British army.

The French sent Willy's younger brothers, Miksha and David, to Drancy. Both boys were in their twenties, and were never seen again.

With the terrifying possibility of Nazi imprisonment, people made desperate decisions. Willy's parents heard about a group of American Quakers passing through the area to pick up two hundred gentile orphans whom they hoped to transport safely to America. Willy's father made certain that his two youngest children joined the group. Ten-year-old Otto, and thirteen-year-old Hilda left their parents and traveled by ship to Baltimore via Casablanca. In the United States, they were placed in Jewish foster homes for the duration of their youth.

In December 1941, the German army was only twenty miles from Moscow. Hitler felt he was so close to victory that he declared "I can see Moscow through my binoculars. In days it will be ours."

He spoke too soon. A propitious cold front — the strongest in thirty years — hit the battlefields. Everything turned to mud, and then to ice. Everything froze, even the German tanks. The fierce cold was tolerable to the Siberian soldiers, who were accustomed to such conditions, but the Germans seemed to weaken with each degree the thermometer dropped. So with nature as a powerful ally, the Siberians finally gained the upper hand. Though Germany would not begin her actual retreat until the following winter, this marked one of Hitler's first real defeats since the Battle of Britain.

Unfortunately, the setback in Russia did not affect the Nazi occupation of Belgium. Willy watched Antwerp change. Jews were required to wear a yellow Star of David on their coats, and the formerly friendly masks of the German soldiers began to wear away as the truth about their mission became widely known. To Willy, as odd as it had been to find that the Germans had become enemies, it was even more bizarre to watch his own countrymen join their ranks. Many Belgian gentiles joined forces with the Nazis with a lifelong commitment.

In August 1942, Willy's problems really began. A German major, Wilhelm Neher, came into the studio. Willy was out, and the major found only Esther and her two daughters. He announced that the studio was no longer their property, and left papers, translated into Flemish, French, and German, so there could be no question about the matter. "Once a month, your husband must come with his books to the Gestapo. This studio is now the property of the German government."

She told him her husband was a Czech, and though she was British by birth, she was also claiming Czech citizenship. He tried to tell her she should claim to be English.

Twice he said firmly, "You are English!"

He knew she had a chance as an English citizen because the British weren't being taken, but why he wanted to help save her life remains a mystery.

When Willy returned home and heard of these newest demands, he turned around and went right back onto the streets. To some, independence is a state that can be lost or altered. To my father, it was so integrated into his being that he knew he would never be able to live under the new, even more oppressive conditions. He hired a smuggler that very night. Unaware of the gravity of his own parents' situation in unoccupied France, Willy had decided to try and join them. He told Esther's parents of his plan, explaining that the trip would be more dangerous with the two children, and pleaded with them to take the older child for the time being. But for reasons that were never clear, my grandmother refused.

Feeling they had no other choice, Willy and Esther placed four-year-old Katie with a gentile family. During the five days in which Willy and Esther prepared to travel, tiny Katie cried constantly. Her young parents visited daily and peered through a window at their daughter's suffering. The baby's relentless hysteria was so great that welts formed all over her face. No longer able to stand her pain, they took her back — a decision that would live on as one of my father's most haunting regrets.

Chapter Five

The Letter — Mirele

"Nothing will ever be the same," Mirele thought as they walked back onto Kievits Straat.

Within days it became obvious what changes had occurred since the huge, chaotic, and failed exodus of the refugees. Mirele's own cousin, Timmy, had been killed somewhere along the road during the erratic gunfire. Willy's sister, Linka, who had also fled on these roads, had lost her arm in the same senseless shootings. Many of the usual neighborhood faces were gone, some never to be seen again. The hope was always that they had gotten on the boats to England, as Fanny and her husband had, but there was enormous uncertainty. Regardless, these were streets filled with a people who had always struggled, and this was just one more chapter in their life stories.

As with Willy, Mirele's daily routine soon seemed almost back to normal. Her father, Chaim, reopened his second-hand clothing shop and she went back to work, although she did decide to seek out a position closer to home. She secured a similar salon job with a smaller Jewish shop in the quarter. Work at Monsieur Jellin's salon on nearby Province Straat was usually uneventful but helped pass the days.

Though many of the familiar faces were now gone, Mirele still spent much time with her old friends who had remained. In a short time, she began to date a young man she'd known from the Youth Club since childhood. With the heightened emotions of war, the romance grew quickly. So, by seventeen, in the midst of all the uncertainty, Mirele had already chosen her husband — whether he had known it or not. Ezryl (Izi) Anielewicz was a tall and extremely handsome young man, a cousin of Mordechai, who would soon gain fame as the leader of the Warsaw Ghetto Uprising. Izi was one of nine brothers, only four of whom would survive the war.

Though tension was high and travel dangerous, Mirele somehow convinced her mother to let her attend a close friend's birthday celebration in Brussels. She traveled by train with her best girlfriend, Madeleine Gotheimer, along with Leon Bulka and Izi.

When the two boys went to check into the hotel, Mirele quickly turned to Madeleine. "Remember, you don't know Leon nearly as well as I know Izi," Mirele warned, "so don't you go doing what I'm going to do."

The two eighteen-year-old girls giggled through the rest of the conversation until they were finally rejoined by their young male companions. Possibly with the threat of deportation fueling them, the night was spent full of love, and thoughts and words about the future, even in a time when the future could seem only a dream. But to young lovers, it always is.

Tragically, Madeleine was deported soon after. She was sent straight to the makeshift brothels set up at the front, and rumors of the abuse she suffered at the hands of the Nazi soldiers prior to her murder were devastating. Years after the war, my mother would tell Madeleine's sister, Jeanne, of the giggles and the love that she'd experienced that night in Brussels, and her sister would cry for melancholy joy.

"I'm so happy... I never knew," she wept, on hearing that her baby sister had at least experienced love before the torture and death that befell her.

Almost immediately after the teens returned home from the

short Brussels excursion, phenomenally perceptive but not much of a romantic, my grandmother Souria quickly made it clear that if Izi wanted to see my mother again, it was only to be as her husband. He ran from this order, as would any young man, but the first time he stood beside a dance floor and watched Mirele in the arms of others, he strode right up to her and proposed.

Though the curfew had curbed much of their social activities, the youth group managed to continue their weekly dances. They would meet at the outskirts of town in a large house now strangely empty following its family's deportation. And when this became too risky, they decided to chance attending a local dance hall — an idea they would all too soon regret, because within minutes of their arrival, ten German *Feldgendarmer* (police) stormed the room.

"Everyone, get into a circle. Make a circle, now!" they ordered.

Everyone in the room nervously began to follow the order.

"Now... every Jew, take three steps forward," the second command came.

The teens did as they were told, while thinking of all their friends already deported.

"Papers!" the Germans demanded.

Again the teens followed orders and presented these German police with identity papers — all of which were immediately confiscated.

"You will come to the station to reclaim these in two days," were the last remarks from the uniformed men as they filed out of the room.

The terrified teens did as ordered, most of them sure they would never return home. Surprisingly, they all reclaimed their papers, and along with them a false sense of security.

My mother and Izi were married behind my grandfather's store in the extremely large kitchen that had once serviced their restaurant, surrounded by the friends and family that remained. My mother wore a beautiful white silk-satin gown borrowed from a friend, and held a simple bouquet of calla lilies. They celebrated the union as if it would have a future, and my father memorialized the occasion of his sister-in-law's wedding with a perfect portrait of the young lovers. The newlyweds began their lives together in the neighborhood in a rented room in the house of an elderly couple, Madame and Monsieur Del Croix. Mirele was already well known by Madame Del Croix — the room was the same one that Esther had once lived in with Willy before the birth of their children presented a need for larger quarters, and Mirele had always been a frequent visitor there.

But tragically, marital bliss was short-lived, for within only three months, Izi came home to find a letter demanding that he report immediately to the Gestapo at the nearby train station. A similar letter had gone out to most Jewish men and women between the ages of sixteen and thirty-five, requiring that they report for work duty. Strangely, most of my mother's friends received one, but somehow, it missed her.

The addressees were ordered to bring one small bag. So, after Mirele and Izi packed his, he put on his jacket, the mandatory yellow Star of David prominent on his chest, and they left for the station. There, at Gare Central off Pelican Straat, among throngs of confused and nervous travelers, Izi kissed his loving child-bride goodbye and was deported to the "work camps."

Mirele's head pounded. Maybe it had been her youth, or simply denial, that had somehow kept her going, and had helped her keep her eyes closed. But now her eyes were forced open, and what she saw was a train leaving the station with her young love and dozens of friends. She started walking, feeling her pace

50

quicken with each step. When she finally got outside the station, she began to run and didn't stop till she reached her older sister's small apartment. There, Esther and Willy comforted her as she wailed uncontrollably. The tears were endless, and the pain and uncertainty more profound than anything she'd ever experienced in her young years.

Meanwhile, still barely eighteen, Mirele gave up the small apartment and returned home to her room above her father's shop. But now, with Izi and all the others gone, things seemed to be getting worse with each day that passed. She waited for the letter that would demand her own deportation. But, luckily, it never came.

Chapter Six

A Train to Hell — Willy

Antwerp, August 8, 1942

My father went to a shoemaker and asked him to put a three-carat diamond into the heel of his shoe.

"Carve a hole and add enough extra heel that it shouldn't wear down," he instructed.

He then methodically packed a large basket with some irreplaceable belongings, which included photo albums, and his and his families' authentic passports. He quickly took this over to his old friend, Madame Del Croix, for safekeeping, and she kindly stored the basket in her attic. The passports he hid inside a wooden window seat in her home.

Willy locked the door of his studio, leaving everything exactly as it was — equipment, photographs, and ten thousand negatives that represented his life's work, none of which he would ever see again. Willy, Esther, Katie, and baby Germaine now met the smuggler, with whom he had made arrangements several days before. With their actual passports hidden, and the appropriate false identity papers in hand, they traveled by train as a gentile family.

When the train reached the French border station, the Gestapo and SS required all passengers to disembark and show their papers. Willy held Germaine in his arms, with Esther and Katie close beside him. Suddenly he noticed that one German officer had focused on him from afar and was heading directly toward him. His stomach leapt to his throat, but he remained stone calm.

"*Papieren*," the officer barked.

Willy calmly took out and handed the soldier his family's false papers.

The officer studied them. My father watched intently as he tried to lift the photograph seemingly in an attempt to discover their secret, but was miraculously satisfied with the authenticity.

Though Willy remained composed throughout the interchange, within five minutes after the officer walked away, perspiration began to pour uncontrollably from his every pore. Within seconds, my father's clothing hung drenched upon his torso, his body's testament to the peril he and his innocent family were facing.

The plan was to travel to Angoulême, a town on the demarcation line between France's occupied and unoccupied zones. Willy and his family successfully reached the city at five o'clock in the morning. But their luck ended there. That same day, there had been a test landing of the Allies — Canadians, Americans, French, and English. Nine thousand soldiers were in Dieppe on the French coast of the Channel. A third of these military men were taken prisoner, a third killed, and a third returned safely to England. Dieppe was the station for German submarines in France, the very submarines that were sinking huge numbers of Allied ships daily, making it an extremely strategic landing for the Allies and a precarious one for the Germans. The Allies' plan had been to blow up the German installation, but they succeeded only in part. Germans were now searching everywhere for their hidden enemies. And at the Angoulême station, they became particularly suspicious of the arrival of over thirty Belgians.

My father had no idea that the smuggler had arranged for so

many refugees to be traveling at the same time, and would never have gone on the journey if he had known this. As they were shuffled off the train, Willy and Esther were separated. Standing with her infant and small child, Esther was approached by a member of the Gestapo.

"*Papieren,*" he demanded.

Esther never became defensive, but instead fussed with a large cross that hung around her neck, while complaining angrily of their detainment. She talked endlessly about the fact that her family was waiting for her and would be worried sick, and that her children were hungry. All the while, she motioned to my father that he should run.

"How could I leave her and the children?" he thought, remaining close by.

Meanwhile, the German she'd engaged in conversation spoke to a member of the French police (now Gestapo collaborators and in charge of the search) on her behalf. He insisted that she was obviously a gentile, but the Frenchman was unyielding. Her signals to Willy continued, but were heeded instead by their smuggler. He and his father ran through the kitchen and out of the station to safety, leaving to their own devices all those who had entrusted him with their lives.

The entire group was taken to a small building. One by one, they would be escorted to the commissar's office on the second floor for interrogation. United only by unfortunate circumstance, none of the group had ever seen one another before. Suddenly, there they were, forced to rely on each other's instincts and intelligence, and to work as a team.

While together, they chose the first to be interrogated. After all, this individual would possibly determine their fate. Consensus fell upon a fifty-year-old gentlemen. Calm, refined, and more educated then most of the others, he was the obvious choice. They sat for what seemed an eternity, anxiously awaiting his return. Unfortunately, the instant he did, they knew their confidence had been far too generously bestowed.

"The commissar is a fine man," the gentleman explained. "I've told him we are Jews with false papers, and he assured me we would all be safe."

Some were irate. Some panicked. Some were somber. Regardless, everyone knew that their fates had been sealed. When the time came for Esther and Willy to meet with this "fine" man, Esther became extremely emotional.

"My husband is an artist," she pleaded. "He cannot be imprisoned. We've heard that they will kill us in Poland."

He seemed to be listening to her and excused himself for a moment to speak with someone outside the office. Esther pointed to an open window and implored her husband to jump. Possessing an artist's soul and being the gentlest of men, she was terrified that he would never survive the camps. But, as in the train station before, my father stood frozen. She continued to prompt him, but his only response was once again the wonderment at the mere thought of abandoning his small family.

Soon, the entire group was moved to the local French prison. And here again, they were taken, one by one, to talk to the German officer who oversaw the prison. One of the first to be interrogated was a young man who stumbled back into the group horribly beat up, cut and swollen — a strong example set to successfully instill fear in the small crowd of captives.

When Willy and Esther were called in, Willy again tried to implore the officer to let them go.

"My wife and the children are British."

The argument had become a mantra that my father chanted over and over to whomever would listen, as if it could conjure the magic needed to save them. And in the years following the war, the chanting continued as if it would wake him from his greatest nightmare.

Willy admitted to having listened to the forbidden BBC. He told the officer that he knew they would be killed if deported. But the officer turned a deaf ear, claiming the words were only propaganda on the part of the Allies.

"Empty your pockets," the officer insisted, and they put their money and whatever else they might have had onto his desk before being sent back down to rejoin the others.

The group remained in the prison for a day and a night. All thirty-five of those taken from the train two days earlier now traveled more than a hundred miles by bus. The trip came to an end at Poitiers, where an old French prison had now been converted into a concentration camp just outside the town. The Poitiers prison was now run by the French police and overseen by the Germans.

There were already approximately one hundred people in the camp. Joined by this new group, it wouldn't be long before there were enough prisoners to make it economically effective to transport them out. The business of genocide was now in full swing — civilians without civil liberties, prisoners who'd never committed a crime, and *murder* as Hitler's "Final Solution."

Being incarcerated, encircled with barbed wire, surely affects people in different ways. Some may become hopeless. Some angry. Either emotion can render them helpless. The Holocaust Jews have been endlessly chastised for walking into the hands of their enemy, walking into the ovens — but does persuasion at gunpoint offer many alternatives for the average man, woman, or child?

Debrouillard is a French word that would best describe the young man, Willy, who had reared himself into successful adulthood. It means to boil or bubble through trouble or circumstance and end up on top — someone who always finds a way. So, to my father, this barbed wire didn't conjure hopelessness, but the contrary.

First, it solidified the reality of the BBC warnings. No more masks. No more charade.

Second, it elicited one goal — the need to escape.

Willy made friends with a French policeman, imploring him to smuggle wire-cutters into the encampment. But the otherwise congenial man refused the request with terror in his eyes.

"May you and God forgive me," he pleaded in a whisper to Willy. "Please don't ask me to do this. Other police, and even one civilian, have already been killed by these German bastards for attempting to help prisoners."

During the weeks in Poitiers, my father studied the confining fence for some weak spot. He also noted that there were always two German watchmen posted beside it. Finally, having decided on the safest location from which to attempt his escape, and awaiting the day he'd acquire a tool to facilitate it, Willy would walk the entire length of the fence each night. Every night but one. The next morning when he went to that same spot, he found that someone else had had the same idea as he: A hole had been cut through, and as he stood there staring at it, Willy imagined that he too had managed to escape.

He had walked by in the middle of the night and seen them with their wire-cutters. They noticed him, then proceeded with a nod that said, "Come with us. Come now." He gestured that he needed a moment and had quickly gathered Esther and their daughters. One by one, he helped them through the hole, finally following himself. They ran into the night... to safety.

But that was just imagination. In reality, he stood numbly staring at the fence. Now boarded up and guarded nonstop, the perfect exit had lost its anonymity. Willy's head reeled. The one night he'd missed was the night he might have stumbled upon the newly cut opening in the fence, a miraculous porthole to his family's survival. But it was the one night he'd missed. Again, he cursed the luck that had evaded them.

A close friend of Willy's, who was also imprisoned in the holding camp, had a gentile wife who visited frequently. During one such visit, it was announced that children could leave if someone was willing to take them. Willy begged the friend's wife to save his babies, but she refused. He then implored her to bring wire-cutters that could allow her husband and his own family to escape. She returned the next day empty-handed.

After about three weeks, Willy's family and some twenty-five other prisoners were taken by van several hundred miles north. Just outside Paris, the Germans had converted a low-income housing facility into another camp — Drancy — a large structure designed to house about ten thousand people. And from here, trains to Poland departed every day. One thousand innocent civilians boarded these transit trains daily.

Even more shockingly, people were being brought into Drancy as fast as they were being deported. General Pétain was a full-fledged collaborator, but now, on a much grander scale, he continued to send refugees from France's unoccupied zone by the droves. Some were Jews, some communists... all considered a worthwhile trade by Pétain for French prisoners that the Germans would happily liberate in exchange.

As the new prisoners arrived, Willy found several familiar faces. They told him that his father had managed to avoid deportation by showing his Hungarian papers. For the time being, since Hungary was a German ally until 1944, the Germans had made a strategic decision to leave the Hungarians alone. For the time being....

Having witnessed the release of several English prisoners, Willy got word of his family's plight to Georges De Groote, still back in Antwerp. He imposed upon Georges what he believed would be a lifesaving deed — to visit Madame Del Croix and secure Esther's and the children's authentic British passports from the window seat where Willy had hidden them. Willy told De Groote that with the passports in hand, he was certain that his wife and the children would be released.

Georges immediately did as requested, but the timing could not have been worse. The evening before there had been a *razzia* — a horrifying and violent SS swarming into the Antwerp quarter, and although the elderly Del Croix couple were gentiles and therefore left physically unharmed, they witnessed the violent taking of an entire Jewish community by these crazed soldiers. When Georges appeared on their doorstep, they were still in shock as he requested they allow him to search for the hidden passports. Trembling, they refused to allow him into the apartment and begged him to leave them alone. Fear of the SS paralyzed them and prevented them from ever allowing him in, though he returned time and time again.

Meanwhile at Drancy, four-year-old Katie broke out in a rash from the filth and was put into the infirmary by her parents. The policy at Drancy was to not separate families for transport — one of the many ruses used to perpetuate the fantasy that all would be fine at the final destination. The longer the fantasy lived, the easier the deportation process, and the better-oiled the genocide machine. Willy insisted that Esther leave Katie in the infirmary as long as possible, biding time as he searched for a miracle. His heart sank the day he glanced out the window and saw his wife returning with their child; with her return, he feared the time for miracles was running out.

About two days later, while Esther was searching for food late in the afternoon, a woman entered their barrack, an area that housed about 30 people.

"Is there an English or American here?" she demanded.

"My wife and daughters are all English," Willy offered anxiously. "They'll be back any second."

"I'm sorry," the woman responded, and she refused to wait.

When Esther returned a short time later, Willy rushed with her to find the woman. Instead, what they found was a locked office. The young couple planned to return the next morning. Assured that freedom was imminent, they made whispered plans long into the night. But their hopes proved false, because at four a.m., in the darkest hour of night, the young family was among the next thousand men, women, and children deported by train to Auschwitz.

Cattle cars they've been called.

When livestock are transported they are treated with a certain amount of respect. They are given food and water. And their car is cleaned periodically during a journey. But not so with the men, women, and children transported by Hitler to the death camps. Whether blue-collar worker or wealthy industrialist, doctor, lawyer, or artist, they were all treated with the same inhumanity. Inhumanity, a one-word oxymoron, and therefore a most peculiar word, to describe what humans are actually capable of.

The car from Drancy was crowded and hot. The complaints of the aged were drowned out by the cries of the children — food, water, or some kind of impossible comfort from their helpless parents. And the stench was unbearable. A mass of people packed like sardines with one bucket that was full of excrement much too soon.

Each car had one large sliding door that was bolted from the outside, and a window less than three-quarters of a meter square. The window was laced with barbed wire, apparently one of the Nazis' favorite materials.

"You must escape," Esther implored Willy once again.

And with her words, he began to work the wires that blocked the window opening. He worked them until his hands bled. He worked them until he was able to climb out. And while beginning that climb, he knew, once again, he could never leave her and the children.

Willy climbed back down.

Esther looked at him desperately, "Go. Please."

But Willy's eyes made clear his decision.

"If you won't, I will," came the voice of his friend, Henri Kramarz. So, instead of his own climb to freedom, Willy helped his friend, and Henri jumped the train that night, and eventually survived the war.

As the train continued into the night, there was a quiet between Willy and Esther. They both looked up at the window periodically, knowing it might hold a last chance for Willy... but an impossibility for Esther or the children. There were occasional periods of silence among the captives... that's when they were most conscious of the humming of the train on the tracks, and the feel of the miles traveled vibrating under their feet — pulling them further and further from the lives they knew, and the people they loved.

The train stopped not long afterward, just 20 miles from the border, in Cologne, Germany. It was now daylight, and the September heat became unbearable. The space in the car allowed for only two or three people at a time to sit and rest. The remainder stood, using one another for support.

My father's fourteen-month-old daughter, Germaine, was sweating profusely. Each time she heard someone relieving himself into the communal bucket, the sound of the liquid against the tin prompted her to beg her helpless parents for something to drink. On one occasion, she was crying while the train was stopped, and Willy noticed several German nurses carrying large buckets of water to the soldiers. He begged them for a drop.

"For the children," he pleaded.

The young women turned a deaf ear. Willy couldn't help hoping it was fear that made them do it — that they were following orders with the threat of punishment, or worse yet, death. It was too horrifying to imagine that these women — who had chosen the profession of healing — could ignore the pleading of suffering children. But maybe they too were suffering... inflicted with the monstrous insanity that seemed to have taken over their entire nation. An insanity that Willy was just beginning to understand, had caught on and was spreading like one of history's most infectious diseases. A plague that manifested slowly at first, starting with a young nurse denying water to a thirsty, dehydrated child, and culminating in acts of inhumanity to man with an intensity and scope that would boggle the mind for decades to come. Inhumanity so unbelievable, in fact, that future historical revisionists would all too often succeed in denouncing it as impossible lies.

The train began to move again, leaving the station at Cologne. With it, left any hope of water... of breathable air... or possibly, of survival.

Three days passed. Three nights. My father has never been able to find the words to really describe those days. The unbearable heat, surpassed only by the intolerable stench. The incessant moaning of the old. The whimpering and wailing of the young.

And then the train finally came to a stop in Kozel. The large cattle door was thrown open. Disorienting light blinded and

63

shocked the ill-fated passengers. And the screaming....

"*Heraus!*" the soldiers yelled in German monster-like guttural howls.

"*Jederman zwischen fünfzehn und fünfzig Jahren. Raus! Raus!*"

"All men between fifteen and fifty. Out! Out!" And with the barked commands came the soldiers, pushing with large police batons. And pulling. And hitting all the male passengers between the years of fifteen and fifty as they jumped from the car — boys and men torn violently from their parents, their wives, their children. Many wonder why the Jews and other prisoners didn't fight at these moments. But the screaming was so loud, and the glaring light from large floods so bright, that there could be nothing but shock after having been holed up in the surreal, dark, moving hell for so many days.

The soldiers began clubbing whoever was closest to the door to punctuate their orders. And though there was no resistance, due to the prisoners' disorientation, the clubbing occurred nonetheless. The soldiers brutally battered every man and man-child they could reach as he jumped from the car. Once out of the car, these unarmed and travel-weakened civilians faced military firearms and young Nazis hungry to utilize them.

"Why didn't you fight?" remains the most common question asked.

"How could we?" is the only obvious and most defendable response.

Still cornered under the window at the back of the car, my father had only an instant to grab his few things, which included a small amount of toiletries. He remembers trying to say good-bye. Katie was screaming so loudly he didn't even hear the guards. Only her cries.

"Daddy, Daddy, please don't leave me here!" she wailed.

Her words echoed over and over in his head as he was pulled from the cattle car.

"Daddy, Daddy, please don't leave me here!"

The pain of leaving this loving child, who, only a month before, had clung to his leg as he worked in his small artist's studio, was so great that something in his brain simply shut down. He would remember absolutely nothing that occurred during the ensuing twenty-four hours.

The following day, a friend from Belgium, who'd been an unfortunate fellow traveler on this catastrophic journey, recounted to Willy what they'd experienced once they were violently taken from that cattle car. He explained in detail that they had stood there for twenty minutes. That Esther had thrown Willy his coat through the hole he'd opened in the barbed wire of the small window. And that the men were then taken in trucks to a camp named Ottmuth.

Ottmuth was another assembly camp. It was cleaner than Drancy had been, and the food was better. The men were relieved and momentarily hopeful.

"Maybe the rumors were wrong. Maybe the Germans were okay after all," they prayed. "Maybe our mothers, wives, and children are doing fine."

Soon after their arrival, the men were given a cup of ersatz coffee, the wartime substitute made from chicory. They hadn't drunk a drop of liquid in three days, and they marveled at how good the beverage tasted.

Brown, a young college student from Antwerp, whose father had owned a shoe store across the street from Studio Willy, recognized my father as he came into the camp. Brown and his father had been in Ottmuth for about a month. The young man was lucky because he was educated, and had been chosen to work in the office as a secretary.

65

His position gave him access to certain favors, and soon after my father's arrival, the young man managed to bring him a bowl of soup. As good as the chicory had tasted, the soup was better yet. Nothing in Willy's past or future could ever compare with that soup. But strangely, my father never saw Brown again. Word came to him later that the father and son both survived the torturous years in the camps only to perish on the death march that was ordered just prior to liberation.

French Jews on the outside had been able to bring blankets and rubber boots to the male prisoners in Drancy. But now in Ottmuth, where the masquerade was most certainly over, the new prisoners were ordered to relinquish them. The barked orders were part of a strategy used to constantly keep the prisoners off-balance as they were forced to stand obediently in line.

"Blankets here!" They pointed to one pile.

"Boots there!" They pointed to another. "For our men at the front."

The previous winter, so many German soldiers had frozen to death on the Russian front that the Nazis were taking no chances this time.

My father had the coat Esther had thrown him from the train. He quickly hid the boots in its sleeves. His blanket he managed to toss onto a nearby laundry line.

He and the other men were sent to barracks. There, they found three tiers of bunks that lined each wall. Willy chose one on the bottom, and carefully hid his boots beneath it. The blanket he miraculously retrieved soon after, and hid under the light cover atop his bunk.

As soon as my father got his bearings, he located the Jewish elder, who happened to be a fellow Czech, and immediately fired a barrage of questions at the man.

"We arrived on the train from Kozel. They took us off, and the train continued to Auschwitz. My wife is English... with my two children. There was no time to show papers, but I told her to yell that she is British." My father asked desperately, "Did she have any chance of survival?"

"I'm in contact with Auschwitz and know everything that is happening there," the elder explained methodically.

"The camp was already overcrowded. That train your family was on went straight to the gas chambers... no one survived." Then, after a beat, "Not even the usual selection."

Whatever the elder's words, Willy refused to lose hope that dreadful day. How could he? Love would never allow it, for as long as there was hope, his wife and babies were still alive. And the truth remained, they were far too young to be dead.

He had reminded Esther so many times to speak out.

"Yell to them that you are British," he'd begged her.

He prayed that she had called out her nationality, and that she and his beloved daughters had been miraculously pulled from death's arms. But his prayers, unfortunately, did not make it so. Although Willy's hope and plans to aid his young family would live on for months, twenty-three-year-old Esther, four-year-old Katie, and fourteen-month-old baby Germaine were all sent straight to the gas chamber.

Chapter Seven

Goodbye to Antwerp — Mirele

Antwerp, Autumn, 1942

Willy, Esther, and the children had been gone for just a couple of weeks when Mirele and her parents were disheartened to receive a card from them explaining they had been taken to Drancy.

Mirele's older sister, Riva, had fled and was now living in a refugee camp in Morocco with her husband and newborn son, Samy. Though far from the gunfire, they remained victim to the ravages of war nonetheless. Childbirth had been treacherous, and with no one to perform an episiotomy, the new mother struggled in pain for weeks, torn and unsutured after a difficult delivery. Food was scarce, and although undernourished herself, she nursed her son for more than two years. When polio spread through the camp, her precious child lay victim, and she literally gave him her blood regularly, keeping him alive and eventually bringing him back to health.

Mirele's brother Benny had taken off again and was living somewhere in Brussels, as was her second brother, Itzhak, with his own young wife. Mirele's mother, Souria, was becoming more and more tense with each day that passed. Having survived the Russian pogroms at the turn of the century, she was no stranger to the inhumanities that might befall them. She knew that trying to tell Benny what to do was a waste of time, but when she heard that Itzhak's wife had been deported, knowing that with war there were no tomorrows, Souria insisted that her husband bring her younger son back to Antwerp.

"Chaim, you bring me my Itzhakla," she demanded. "*Yetz.* Now. Go to Brussels and bring home our boy."

Chaim knew better than to argue with my grandmother when her mind was set. Two decades later, after they'd moved to Los Angeles, one of my greatest amusements would be to watch him, at age ninety-two, quietly turn off his hearing aid and smile lovingly as she criticized with enormous zeal, sometimes at the top of her lungs, one of his mischievous misdeeds. But in 1942, aged seventy and with his hearing still intact, he had little choice but to listen, so he departed for Brussels immediately. He collected Itzhak in no time and was on the train back to Antwerp when it made a stop near Malines. Malines, like Poitiers, was a newly adapted assembly camp, which, only a short time before, had been an old military barrack. Before Chaim could do anything to stop him, his son jumped from the train.

"Papa, I have to find her," he tried to explain as the train pulled away. "I have to go to my wife... I can't leave her there alone. She's so young... so frail. She needs me, Papa. My place is with her... we'll be fine if we're together. Tell Mama I love her."

Neither Itzhak nor his wife would ever be seen again.

A few nights later, Mirele was jolted by the sound of guns, screams, and boots pounding on the cobblestones just outside her home. She ran to the same window that had bonded her with her dear friends and watched in terror as every one of them, along with their families, were brutally torn from their homes and pushed into waiting trucks — trucks so cramped that many suffocated to death before arriving at their destination.

My mother and her parents prepared their things and waited in fear for the vicious guards, whose commands echoed from the streets below, to pound on their door as they were pounding on all the others.

They waited.

70

And waited.

And waited.

But the pounding never came. They sat at the table with their few things ready for the transport and listened as the first truck pulled away. And then, the last. They sat at the table quietly and watched night turn to day, finally surmising that the chocolate factory that wrapped around their building and bore a large sign — *Chocolat Beukelaar* — had apparently confused the SS, who had not noticed that there was a residence at its center. Luck.

Mirele looked out the window at the deserted quarter. She quickly slipped out the door and ran across the street to check on the family of her best friend, Madeleine. Madeleine had already been deported, but her sister, Jeanne, and their parents still occupied the apartment just across the street. Mirele quietly slipped into their home and found Jeanne lying in bed with her small newborn child. The traumatized young mother was burning with fever. As Mirele brought her what nourishment and drink she could find, Jeanne weakly told her of the previous night's horrors.

She had been lying in bed, just as Mirele had found her, when the guards stormed into the room. Her parents had run to hide in the chicken coops they kept on the roof of the building, where they were soon discovered and brutally forced down through the apartment and out onto the streets. When they found the young mother burning with fever, an infant in her arms, the two guards began to disagree with each other.

"Get up," one fiercely demanded of the fevered woman. "Now. Put on some clothes."

"Don't bother. Look at her, she's burning up," the second said. "Leave her here. It makes no difference. She'll be dead by morning... the baby soon after."

And they left. But he was wrong. She didn't die that night.

71

Instead, shortly after Mirele's visit, she dressed and took the train to Brussels. There, she found shelter with an aunt and uncle. Unfortunately, only a few weeks later, a neighbor denounced them to the Nazis, and she and her aunt and uncle were loaded into the back seat of a black Citroën. She carried her baby in her arms.

When the car came to a stoplight, she somehow managed to force open the door. It flew open, and she right out of it. She ran down the streets and managed to sneak into a movie theater. There, with her child enveloped in her arms, she hid from her pursuers behind some heavy velvet drapes. After what seemed like an eternity later, her heart still in her throat, she was discovered by a young man. Fortune had found her once again, for the boy was a member of the resistance.

"Don't move," he whispered, "I'll be back to get you."

As promised he returned, and soon after, found sanctuary for her in a home in the countryside. There she remained for the duration of the war... though never to see her sister, her brother Jacques, or her parents again.

Finding no one else on the once-busy neighborhood streets, Mirele returned to her parents' apartment. She joined them at the small dining table, where they all sat quietly, still numb from the night's horror. A knock finally jarred them. When they opened the door they didn't find the Gestapo, but Renée Marion, a young gentile woman who was Benny's newest girlfriend.

Uncle Benny had never lived a day of his life in quiet. He was a gambler, and extremely volatile, but the love for his mother and his sister remained immeasurable, and just as he'd miraculously found them on the border roads a year before, he was now determined to find them again.

"Benny heard what happened last night," Renée said, explaining her surprising arrival. "He's waiting for you now... in Brussels."

"He's ridiculous," Souria put up a fight. "Why Brussels? It's no safer there."

"Safer or not, he's insisted I bring you," Renée continued. And when it appeared that Souria wasn't budging from her stand, the young woman sat herself down and began to cry hysterically.

"Well, if you're staying, then I'm staying right here with you," she explained through her tears. "Benny promised to kill me if I come back without you."

"Don't be ridiculous," Souria responded.

"Really?" She defended. "He even showed me the gun!"

Souria knew Benny would never have shot the young woman, but she also knew fireworks would most certainly fly if Renée returned without them. Moreover, she knew life in Antwerp was over for them.

"Fine, then. Stop that crying and go and fix your face. Mirele, Chaim... get your coats.... There's nothing left for us here."

As they put on their coats, Renée quickly tore the Yellow Stars off them, against my grandmother's protests.

"Benny's orders," she defended her actions as if it were law.

They traveled by train to Brussels. By that evening, Benny had secured them sanctuary with an elderly woman in a two-story brownstone-like home at 16, Rue des Echelles. Madame Abrams was the mother of Warren Abrams, a good friend of Benny's and sometimes partner in his nefarious dealings. Warren was more of an established businessman of sorts, so whenever Benny found himself low on cash, Warren would front him whatever he needed. Benny would then happily split the profits from the ensuing venture, and they both eventually ended up winners.

Warren's gracious mother, who they soon called *Bomma* (Grandma) Abrams, took Benny's family in wholeheartedly. She gave her upstairs bedroom and bed to her guests, and slept through the nights seated at the dining table. She would straddle her chair like a cowboy, arms folded to pillow her head onto the chair back. The more my grandmother protested, the more insistent *Bomma* Abrams became.

"It's not for you," she promised. "It's the only way I can sleep these days. Even if you weren't here I'd be sleeping on this chair. But now I'm fortunate enough to have company."

Chapter Eight

Peiskretscham — Willy

"He who has a 'why' to live for, can bear with almost
any 'how.'"

Nietzsche

Ottmuth to Peiskretscham, September 1942

Ottmuth confined about five hundred men at any given time — a
constant flow of prisoners were moved in and out. Each day,
officials from various "work camps" would come to collect
"workers." They did their best to choose the healthiest and
strongest. Sometimes it seemed they were most interested in the
quality of the boots the prisoner wore. The equation was quite
simple — the man with the best shoes would last the longest. The
men were nothing more than a commodity, standing in lines
waiting to be chosen to advance some Nazi enterprise.
Sometimes they were to be used as slaves to work for
government projects like transportation or telephone systems.
Sometimes local factories and entrepreneurs happily paid the
German government for their labor — companies as familiar as
Krupp, Mercedes, and even America's well-established Ford
Corporation's German factory profited from the use of unpaid
slave labor. Often as young as 14 years of age, these slaves were
forced into learning factory skills in record time with the threat
or actuality of a violent beating if they didn't — the violent
beatings frequently culminated in murder.

Soon after his arrival at Ottmuth, my father and his friend

were picked, along with a hundred other men, and put on trucks destined for Peiskretscham, a camp located on the German-Polish border in Upper Silesia. Although the Germans affectionately called it a work camp, the fact that men were worked without sufficient nourishment until they died led its residents to label it more appropriately a "death camp."

Willy met another young man on the transport truck. His hands were in fine shape and showed no signs of work.

"What do you do back home?" Willy asked.

"I'm a student. Of medicine."

There were students and lawyers, manual laborers and intellectuals, pious men and atheists, rich and poor. So, in fact, the only thing most of these men had in common was that they had been free only months before, and now were doomed.

It was September 1942 when the truck with Willy entered Peiskretscham's barbed-wire fences. The new arrivals observed a long line of prisoners holding small metal boxes used as plates. It was dinnertime. They had just completed a long and difficult day of work and were being given their only sustenance for the evening — a watery soup. If they were held in favor by the person ladling out the broth, they might get a portion from the bottom of the pot that potentially included some small remnants of the few peas and potatoes used to create the concoction.

Willy recognized several faces from Antwerp.

"How long have you been here?" he asked one man whose worn clothing hung like rags from his skeleton-like frame.

"One month," the man responded.

"Only one month," my father thought with horror, "and he looks like death. They all look like living corpses. Nothing but bones."

He was terrified.

Each of the prisoners watched the new arrivals, looking for a familiar face. One Kapo emerged from amongst them and walked directly to Willy, affectionately throwing his arms around him. Willy didn't remember ever having seen the man before.

"Willy. You took my girlfriend's photograph. Do you remember her?"

People often connected with those they'd barely known back home as if they were long lost friends. After all, any connection could help take the slightest edge off the nightmare they were now living, even for the Kapos. And the memory that connection would conjure up might help them through one more day.

Kapos won the reputation as the scum of the war. Prisoners who worked as foremen for the Nazis, the Kapos would mercilessly beat their compatriots into submission. Willy did not see this man, this Kapo, again for weeks. But the surprise Willy felt at the embrace of this veritable stranger was only surpassed by his shock at their next meeting a month later.

The man entered my father's barrack. He was screaming, as was the way of most Kapos, functioning only through intimidation.

"We're looking for blankets," he barked. "We know one of you has one."

He checked each bed quickly but carefully, each prisoner standing obediently beside his bunk. The knowledge of his own cache had Willy's heart pounding, though tempered slightly by the recollection of the Kapo's affectionate embrace upon his arrival. When he stopped at Willy's bunk, the man soon discovered the woolen blanket hidden beneath my father's covers.

"It's you!" he screamed, as he hit Willy so hard that bells rang in his ears.

As my father recovered from the blow, he wondered what could make a man capable of becoming such a heinous watchdog for his captors. He knew that if survival in the camps required this enormous loss of humanity, he had to get out, and there was not a moment of any day that his mind didn't work toward escape.

Each morning he would stand in line with the other prisoners. The first day there, they had been asked if there was a doctor among them. No one responded. Willy stood beside the young medical student he'd met on the truck. He gave him a slight shove.

"Tell them you're a doctor," Willy insisted in a whisper.

"I'm only a student," he whispered back, too terrified to respond to the Nazis.

The following day they asked again, "Is there a doctor here?"

Once again Willy prodded. And once again the young man refused. He knew that this frail young man with the fine white hands would never survive manual labor, so with a strong sudden shove, my father attempted to push him to survival. He forced the young medical student forward in a way he couldn't jump back. The result for the young man seemed miraculous. He was immediately given a small barrack infirmary and a bunk for himself.

But in Hell nothing can be truly good. The Nazis had special orders for this young doctor's infirmary. He was told to do what he could to cure the sick... but only for twenty-four hours. If by the end of one day they were not ready to return to work, he was to kill them by injection. His own life would depend on his ability to carry out this order.

That same first day, the German officers told the prisoners that the camp was building a storage facility for potatoes.

"Who is a locksmith?" they demanded.

A Frenchman stepped forward and was taken to work.

"Who knows how to lay bricks?" they demanded.

My father knew that surviving meant being useful, so he too stepped forward. He had grown up on a farm where there was little outside help. Though a professional photographer, he luckily had been home-taught in most crafts.

Hours later, as Willy worked with the others on the walls of the structure, the head of the camp walked by to examine their efforts. He stopped beside the locksmith, who was having an extremely difficult time with his chore.

"What are you doing?!" the officer screamed furiously.

Surmising the man had never worked a lock, the guard began to beat him. Willy stood frozen. He had never seen anything like this in his life. The violence was beyond comprehension... and the young man's blood poured out onto every surface in testimony.

Willy wondered at his nightmare fate, but his thoughts quickly moved to his beloved wife and children. If they were alive, and he wanted to believe they were, he would escape this insanity and secure their papers.

He watched himself taking the English papers to the Swiss consul who represented the English in wartime Belgium. He would speak with them and explain everything. They would nod sympathetically. "Something will be done," they would promise. "She'll be home in no time. Leave everything to us." Willy would feel huge relief as he left the consul building knowing it was a matter of days till he would have them back.

A yell nearby woke Willy from the daydream. He returned to his effort to create perfect masonry. As Nietzsche said, "He who has a 'why' to live for, can bear with almost any 'how.'" Saving his family became Willy's reason for living, and with this most profound "*why*" came the ability to withstand even the most horrendous "*how*." And no matter the fear that it might be too late, Willy held true to the smallest and most potent desire to succeed.

Within one or two days, the masonry project completed, Willy rejoined the others that left the camp each day in the predawn hours. Each was given one cup of chicory before departing. In addition, each group of 32 men was given one loaf of bread to divide among them; each one was allocated a tiny piece with a bit of jam. And because they knew this was all they were to be given till nightfall, the men scrutinized the size of each other's portions hungrily to see if there had been any injustice.

Before the sun had risen, they would then begin their somber walk into the countryside; dread, an ominous cloud hovered above their heads. For what seemed to be about three miles, some five hundred men, prisoners, would trudge silently with their heads hung low. When they finally arrived at their worksite, my father learned that they were to help build what was intended to be part of the "Trans-Siberian Railroad." This was an essential element of Hitler's grand plan to control the entire continent.

The prisoners worked in teams of two with beams one foot square and fifteen feet long. My father was partnered with an Austrian, and told to carry the logs. Willy soon learned that the man had bone cancer, making him much too weak to pick up the log.

"Here, let me help you," Willy whispered as he lifted one end onto the man's shoulder, then quickly ran to pick up the other end.

They repeated this routine several times until noticed by a young soldier.

"Stop! He must do it alone!" the soldier yelled at Willy while menacingly pointing a rifle at the older man.

And so Willy's sickly partner began to lift the logs with the greatest of difficulty.

"Have you heard of the Rauff trucks?" the older man asked quietly as they worked.

"No," Willy shook his head, and the man continued.

"They come every two weeks or so. I'm sure you've seen them.... Black metal trucks with two large doors in back?" he looked to his partner for some recognition. "No? Well, they have quite an amazing design. Exhaust pipes go directly into the passenger compartment. Not where the drivers are, of course. They come to pick up those who are too tired, or weak, or sick to work. They go straight to Auschwitz. By the time the trucks reach the camp, they go directly to the crematories. Don't even need to stop at the gas chambers... all the passengers are dead. Very convenient, no?"

Willy worked and listened. The words were as surreal as his life had become. He looked at the quiet man, wishing he could ease his pain.

"I long to be on that truck," the older man confided to my father.

"Every day you live offers a chance for a change... of survival," Willy tried to reassure him.

But optimism was a luxury much too painful for the man to afford. He simply could not face another day in the "work camp," and so death became his only way out.

Willy toiled under the weight of moving these beams for several days before being transferred to construction. Here the weeks went by slowly. The work was hard, and food scarce. Each day at noon, Willy's stomach cried for food, remembering the lunch hour from a time gone by —

Of locking up the shop and going home to his apartment where his wife had prepared a wholesome lunch for him and the girls. Or perhaps they would go to her mother's small restaurant where neighborhood conversation was as plentiful as the delicious food.

He held onto these memories, which soon became his only sustenance while his stomach was forced to forget the past, and become accustomed to the lack of nourishment.

Willy worked under civilian Polish gentiles who were the construction foremen for the project. These men, though paid, had been given mandatory orders to be there and were not fans of their German oppressors.

One day a train arrived, each car carrying 40 tons of *Kiesel stones* (gravel) to make cement. My father and an even younger man were given shovels and told to unload each car within four hours. The temperature had begun to drop, and the unbearable heat soon turned to unbearable cold. The trains would arrive with their load of stones partially frozen together, making the job of unloading them doubly difficult. The two young men were told to shovel the stones out and toss them into piles far from the tracks to avoid any interference with the railcar's wheels.

They struggled for some time. My father worked the way he always had, no matter the challenge — hard and skillfully. His partner, a mere seventeen, was not nearly as strong or skillful. A nearby guard noticed that, unbeknownst to Willy, his side was moving much faster. The guard came seemingly out of nowhere and grabbed the young boy's shovel and began to violently beat the boy with it.

"Too slow!" he screamed. "*Schnell!* Faster."

Maybe it was shock that overtook Willy. Maybe disgust. But whatever feelings he might have had, they were most assuredly accompanied by terror — a fear that pulsed through his every vein. He couldn't help wonder how this beating, weakening the young man with every blow, could help increase efforts. But the horrific truth suddenly crystallized as my father feverishly increased his own efforts threefold. No matter the damage caused to the young boy, his beating had in fact increased work output.

"But for how long?" Willy wondered. All the prisoners were given so little food their bodies quickly lost the nutrients required to survive, let alone to fuel the heavy labor in the "work camp." One evening, Willy witnessed a man returning to the barracks at the end of a workday, his body swollen from head to toe.

"His blood has turned to water," the other men began to whisper amongst themselves.

"He will be dead tomorrow," the whispers continued.

And so he was.

Willy knew he wouldn't be able to survive if he continued at the labor he'd been assigned, so when the request for electricians came, he once again stepped forward.

His new job consisted of wiring the tops of tall telephone poles. Wearing shoes with cleats, he climbed the poles and worked with large wires in the frozen air. The job was more difficult than most, but the need for deft precision, and the reality of the cold, forced the guards to allow Willy and the others to take frequent breaks in order to thaw their fingers. So, though the frostbite was painful and the work grueling, the time to thaw their fingers and hands actually broke the degree of energy output all the other jobs seemed to entail, making this one highly desirable.

"Willy, give them my name," acquaintances would call out as they passed. "Tell them I'm a good worker."

Surrounded by barbed wire and guards with rifles, a prisoner's survival would seem to have depended only upon liberation. But it would probably be more accurate to say that

that survival depended on the hope for liberation. For some, liberation was a vision of the camp walls being thrown over by tanks, with Allied flags flying high, and soldiers taking Nazi guards as prisoners, shooting down those who resisted. Willy had never really relied on anyone his entire life, and this certainly didn't seem to be the time to start. For him, liberation continued to mean escape. So Willy spent every waking — and possibly sleeping — moment planning it. He knew pulling it off would require strength. He'd seen what one short month had done to the prisoners of his camp, and he couldn't afford that kind of weakness. He needed less strenuous work, and soon.

Though the Polish workers were officially paid civilian laborers, their jobs were not done of their own free will. Instead, they worked only through the threat of imprisonment by their German oppressors. They, too, were dreaming of life as it had been, where they could return to mothers or wives after a day of labor, and where the money they earned was commensurate with their output.

Like many Eastern Europeans, my father understood several languages, including the Polish spoken by these civilian workers. He began to speak with them in their native tongue, and whenever he passed them he would sing a Polish tune that he remembered from his youth.

"Poland will not go under so long as we live...."

They applauded the sentiment and liked the young Czech. So, when my father quietly asked that they request his "skilled" assistance, they did just that. Willy reported for duty the following day, and was relieved to learn he had been moved from hard labor to carpentry with the Polish workers — a *lucky* move that most certainly aided in saving his life.

He was the only Jew among the Poles, but always true to form, Willy worked hard and tirelessly. He quickly became an asset, and his optimism was an inspiration to the others. Days moved painfully slowly from one to the next, and as my father became thinner and thinner, his artist's hands became callused, dirt eventually embedded deeply beneath the skin. Fortunately, his mind remained sharp and constantly focused on one thing only — escape.

My father was certain that it was not a comfortable thing for these civilian Polish workers to befriend him. They had freedom; he was doomed. They had food; he was reaching starvation. But with all the horror of war, comes vast opportunity for good, and small acts of kindness often have the ability to change lives, or even save them. No matter how small some of these acts might have been, the enormity of the good inherent in them is increased tremendously with the looming threat of physical punishment or death.

On one particular day, no different than any other, as my father worked beside his new friends he experienced such good. The Poles had a small communal residence on the hill where they were all working. It was there the men ate and slept until their "leave," when they would temporarily return to their families and real homes.

"You!" one man instructed him toughly, and loudly enough for the nearby German guards to hear. "Take this bucket of water up to the house." He then continued in a barely audible whisper, "There is food there, Willy... but you cannot stay one minute because if the Germans see, I will be killed!"

My father followed the order, carrying the bucket into the nearby house. When he entered his eyes went straight to a pot of leftovers that stood atop the stove. There was someone there that had apparently been expecting him, quickly handing him a bowl of cold bean soup. Willy consumed the hearty peasant fare so fast it wasn't really eating at all, but an action that could be more likened to inhaling. Next to the soup pot was a second pot containing five large cooked potatoes.

"Eat them quickly," the saint said.

My father began to eat them whole, one at a time, five large potatoes in five bites. He had always been a rather thin man with a polite appetite. But that man that he had been was now buried inside a starving creature who, within seconds, had consumed more food than he had eaten in months. Food that brought him the strength to keep going, and kindness that brought him faith and courage. No matter how many bean soups he's tried in these last fifty-five years — and the search has been extensive — none has ever tasted as good as that cold soup on that icy day.

With each new agony-filled moment, Willy became more and more determined to escape. Denied sufficient nutrition to survive, planning the escape and rescue of his wife and children became his sustenance. To achieve such an impossible task, he realized he would have to trust someone. Of all the Polish workers he'd grown to know, my father had become especially close to one in particular. When the man mentioned that he was going home for the weekend, my father gave him his own cherished wedding ring, which he had hidden until that moment.

"Please bring me some bread and eggs," he asked, knowing perfectly well that he'd have absolutely no recourse if the ring simply disappeared.

"It was impossible to find eggs," the man told Willy when he returned the following week. "I hope this will help," he added, secretly handing my father a loaf of bread and an onion.

Willy stared at the food in hand, marveling at his good fortune and the kindness inherent in the Pole's gesture.

"Thank you," Willy whispered the understatement from the bottom of his heart as he took the offering.

By this time my father had decided his chances of surviving an escape would be increased if he were joined by strategically chosen companions. To this end, he had begun to plan with another prisoner by the name of Leopold Goldwurm, an electrician from Antwerp. Knowing they'd never make it without food, my father cut the bread and the onion into halves and waited for Leopold to meet him in the barracks that evening. There, in secret, they ate it as fast as possible, well aware others would have killed for such a feast.

Soon after, once the others had returned to the barracks, a look of awe came over another prisoner while talking to my father.

"Willy, you've eaten an onion," he whispered reverently.

My father acknowledged him with a quiet nod.

"Please, please just open your mouth so that I may smell it," the man implored him. "Exhale, Willy. Please. Please exhale."

My father did so, and with eyes closed the man inhaled deeply, imagining he was consuming the greatest meal of his life. And there they stood, barely acquaintances, face to face. One man breathing out; the other breathing in. Closer together in this ritual than even the closest of friends would have ever found themselves in the real world, sharing one more bizarre moment in what had become part of their surreal existence. Sharing the memory of an onion and the meal it conjured.

Now, with even greater trust in the Polish worker who'd brought him the food, my father confided his escape plans. The Pole helped him further by drawing a map in the snow that would guide the escapees to the nearest town — another small act of kindness punishable by death. My father quickly memorized every inch and obliterated the map before anyone else might have noticed it.

There was a nightly head count in the camp, and because my father's plan was to escape at night, he had to devise some means of buying a few extra hours before their disappearance was noticed. So, every evening he went to visit his new friend, the doctor. Therefore, each evening, when the guards came to count the men in the bunk, there were always only 31 instead of the supposed 32. And each evening, someone would say, "Willy is with the doctor."

Making this the norm, my father felt, would buy him the cushion of time needed to gain some distance from the camp before they'd realize he was really gone.

Knowing the escape would require money, my father made the decision to confide of his plan to the doctor as well. He knew this was risky, but trusted the man, especially with the added factor that everyone dreamt of someone successfully escaping. Somewhere inside each prisoner was the hope that if word of their living hell reached the outside world, someone or something would intercede to save them.

Willy worked the heel of his shoe until he reached the diamond he had had built into it a lifetime ago. That evening, when he went to visit the doctor, he brought the stone.

"I need your help," Willy demanded. "This is a perfect three-carat stone. Can you help me sell it?"

"I'm taken each week to a pharmacy," he offered. "I can ask there if someone might be interested."

The doctor did as promised, and when he returned from his next visit, he told Willy that the pharmacist would buy it. My father turned over his treasure. But though he'd confided in his new friend, he did not trust that the young man was beyond temptation. After all, desperate men do desperate things. So, afraid that the doctor would return from the pharmacy saying that he'd lost it before arriving, Willy stressed the importance of insuring the safety of the stone.

"Please be very careful," my father pleaded. "Here, let me

button it into your pocket so that there is no chance it can be lost," he continued, as he placed the stone carefully into the doctor's pocket and buttoned it closed as the man looked on.

When he returned from his next pharmaceutical buying trip, the doctor returned my father's diamond to him.

"The pharmacist said it was too large for him to deal with," the doctor claimed. "Do you have any smaller ones?"

My father knew that his friend Leopold had smaller stones and asked him if he wanted to sell them to get the cash they would be needing. Leopold agreed, and Willy took them to the doctor and repeated the process of putting them safely into his pocket. But this time, upon the doctor's return, my father's fears were actualized.

"Willy, all day I've been looking for the diamonds," he confessed. "I don't understand how I could've lost them."

Sadly, both he and my father knew that his confession was not for the loss, but for the crime of theft against a friend. There was nothing my father could do, no recourse whatsoever. And the doctor knew it. My father believed that the young man had probably wanted to steal that first stone too, but couldn't allow himself to do it if it was the only one Willy possessed. But some strange, rationalized morality allowed the theft of the others. And unfortunately, in doing so, the doctor instilled a new fear in my father. He had always been sure that one of the most essential tools of his escape would be the three-carat stone that the — now clearly untrustworthy — doctor had full knowledge of. Moreover, without cobbler's tools, Willy had no way of returning the diamond to the safety of his shoe heel. He knew he had to find a hiding place for it, and soon.

My father noticed that the handle of his shaving brush unscrewed, and that, on the inside, the fine boar's hair bristles were held in place by wax. Carefully, with his craftsman's hands, he heated the wax and buried the diamond inside. Once the handle was put back on, he felt certain no one would ever suspect it. The consequences of being wrong would have been unthinkable, as the gravity of such a cache was huge. The loss of the diamond would be nothing compared to the punishment.

Every day, Germans of some sort would show up to talk to the prisoners. Sometimes guards. Sometimes officers. They would offer the vulnerable men a loaf of bread for diamonds or dollars, thinking they'd be stupid, desperate, or simply delusional enough to want to believe in their promises. One night they came in, asking for someone by name. A Parisian man stepped forward. He had been a wealthy and successful manufacturer of cord in simpler times, but now he was just another prisoner who had become a very, very old fifty years of age.

"We've heard you have dollars," they demanded.

"I have nothing," the man pleaded.

After months in the camp, he was no longer a strong man, so the beating the Germans inflicted upon him, which would have taken down even the most powerful of men, took its toll quickly. Blood ran freely from every part of his head. The other prisoners, also weakened by starvation and abuse, lay there helplessly as they had been forced to do so many times before. And, as many of their bodies were already near death, the pain of their helplessness destroyed what little was left of their spirits with every blow.

"I have nothing," the defenseless man begged over and over again.

His blood poured from him along with his pleas, but the "men" in search of dollars did not stop until their victim had to be dragged out unconscious. My father never saw the man again. But he did see his murderers a few nights later when they returned.

"Herskovic, William!" they shouted.

My father stepped forward.

"We know you have diamonds!"

My father denied having any stones and somehow remained calm as he was forced to show the men everything in his possession. Three items: a toothbrush, a razor, and... a shaving brush. Slowly they moved these meager items from one pile to another, then back again. My father stood by and watched mesmerized as the three-item pile moved back and forth. He watched his shaving brush move back and forth between these piles and feared the beating that would certainly happen to him if they found the diamond hidden inside it, and possibly a more severe one if they did not. Maybe he was able to hold his calm, sensing some strange fate was preventing the beating from happening even at that very moment, for custom in the camps would have had it so, with his unwillingness to manifest the stone they were sure he had. And the toiletries went back and forth again as if the Germans were waiting for something to suddenly appear in their midst.

"I have nothing," Willy guaranteed, as he'd heard so many other men guarantee before him. Certain a beating was about to ensue, he awaited the first painful blow, making an effort not to look down at the smooth wood that made up the handle of the shaving brush that lay on the bunk before him.

"Nothing," he repeated.

And the items went back and forth. Then suddenly, the men left without ever having raised their hands or batons to him even once. Luck again? It was strange the gratitude my father felt towards the doctor that night. Willy was convinced that the doctor had to have told these guards of his diamond, for how else would they have known? But as angry as he could have been with the young man, their non-physical attack made Willy sure

91

the doctor had solicited a promise that they wouldn't hurt his "friend." Willy could have hated the young doctor for the betrayal, but he chose to be thankful that he wasn't hurt. Somewhere in the act, Willy chose to recognize a twisted kindness, and in the camps any kindness, no matter how small or twisted, was appreciated.

My father knew the importance of friends in the concentration camps, and made sure to collect them where he could. So, after somehow striking up an acquaintance with a German civilian contractor named Arthur Walde, Willy decided to ingratiate himself with Walde senior. An older man, the contractor's father was responsible for the tool shed. It was his job to record who had taken each tool. Willy began affectionately calling him Papa. He knew he'd need Papa's friendship in one way or another, so he visited the man frequently. Whether or not he needed a tool, Willy would go to old Walde and check one out, spending time in cordial conversation with him... and then again when he'd return it. One day, Willy became very aware of the poor condition of Walde's teeth and deduced he might be incapable of eating the hard crust of country bread that he received.

Their friendship had already begun to take shape, so Willy found the courage to ask, "Do you happen to have some crust from your bread? Please don't throw it away if you ever do... please save it for me," Willy continued uncomfortably.

Having worked since childhood, Willy had never been in need and was extremely proud, but near starvation and without the freedom to fend for himself, he found himself reduced to begging. Wordlessly, Walde turned and walked to a battered old tool chest. He opened it and several mice scampered out. Quietly, he pulled six or seven pieces of crust from a shelf. Still without words, he handed them to Willy. My father looked upon the old morsels of bread as though they were life itself — for in fact, that's exactly what they were. He was wearing his winter coat and, using one of Walde senior's tools, cut the pocket carefully and hid his precious "gold" inside the lining.

When he returned to work, he slid his hand through the pocket and into the lining and broke the small morsels into even tinier pieces. These he would take out one at a time and place carefully into his mouth. Never chewing, he would hold them there until they'd dissolve, hoping to enjoy them for the longest possible time.

The almost sacred ritual conjured up a childhood memory that made his work seem just a little easier that day. He remembered being told about "manna from heaven," and that everyone's manna was so incredibly delicious because it tasted like their own particular favorite food. To one, it would be meat. To another, cake. As a young child, Willy had always wondered how that could be true. But suddenly as the small morsel of dried crust, the discard of an old man and a field mouse, began to dissolve in his mouth, Willy knew the legend was true. For this crust suddenly became "manna from heaven," as good as, or better than, anything he had ever tasted. And as his state of starvation had greatly increased by this time, those tiny morsels might have even surpassed the taste of the bean soup he'd had months before.

Chapter Nine

Gloves and Other Things — Mirele

"Chop wood, carry water..."
Ancient Zen saying

Brussels, Winter, 1942

With most hours spent in the confines of her small apartment, the time with elderly *Bomma* Abrams went by very slowly. My grandparents rarely ventured out, and when they did it was usually just for a short stroll in the immediate neighborhood. Though there was a high risk of deportation for any Jew found on the streets, young Mirele wasn't timid. Her will to live, in fact, to live normally, found its expression even in this bleakest of times. Eager to shed her "Semitic" appearance, my mother bleached her dark auburn hair blond, and spent the months that followed focused on survival.

She would pack a small sandwich and take the short train ride from Brussels back to Antwerp each month. Absurd as it may have seemed, with the sandwich in her possession she somehow felt an odd sense of security, knowing that if the Nazis apprehended her, she would at least have one more meal.

Once in Antwerp, she would pick up her family's ration cards, always terrified that the Gestapo might discover that they had changed residence. On one of her first visits, Mirele made it a point to get to know the young clerk who dispensed the cards. As always, her friendliness was contagious.

"You should be more careful," he offered one day. "It's very dangerous here. Look around, there are Gestapo everywhere," he whispered. "They collect Jews whenever they choose... it's really not safe for you."

"Well, I've really no choice," Mirele responded with a frightened voice. "My parents need to eat."

"Then, from now on... don't approach me right away. Walk around. Wait, and look for me to take out my comb. When I run it through my hair, you'll know it's safe. Come to the desk *only* then."

Mirele is convinced that the clerk's simple gesture most certainly contributed to her survival. During these frequent and very necessary trips, Georges De Groote's friendship with our family remained consistent. Every week as Mirele's train would pull into the station, he'd be there. He would then accompany my mother to the ration card bureau. By this time, De Groote had joined the Belgian Police Force in order to avoid working for the Nazis, and his uniform provided just the amount of security she needed beside her as she walked through streets now visibly devoid of Jews. Her fear was justifiably reduced by the presence of this tall Flemish youth, for with Georges, she appeared to be simply half of any anonymous gentile couple — a responsible, law-abiding couple at that. Mission accomplished, Georges would put the very grateful young woman back onto the train to Brussels.

During these dangerous excursions, Mirele sometimes felt that life was actually almost normal. It was hard to believe that, with this kind and handsome young man attentively taking her nineteen-year-old arm, she was actually a married woman whose husband had been taken from her and put into some distant and foreign prison camp. Georges would often tease that his feelings were perhaps stronger than simple friendship, and

96

America

Willy with me and my
sisters, Suzanne & Micheline
(I'm the one on the car)

Willy & Mirele
Bel Air Camera

Me, Suzanne
& Micheline

Suzanne, me
and Mom
(Santa Monica)

Mirele, Patricia, Suzanne,
Micheline & Willy (Vegas)

Pre-War Antwerp

Includes Riva, Souria, Esther, Willy, Mirele, & Armand
Antwerp, 1938

Mirele, Madeleine
& friend

Mirele
Studio Willy portrait

Benny with doll-filled auto

Czechoslovakia

Willy, age 13, with first camera
Self portrait

Willy, age 17

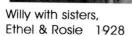

Willy with sisters,
Ethel & Rosie   1928

Willy's grandmother, aunt, mother
& grandfather   circa 1913

Willy's brother, Armand
fled France into Spain
at fifteen

Two years later he was
deported to Israel
where he enlisted in
the Palestinian division
of the British Forces

Willy's brother,
Simon

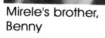

Mirele's brother,
Benny

Willy & Esther's
wedding celebration

Esther
Antwerp,
1939

Willy in studio
Antwerp, 1938

Katie
Antwerp, 1941

Esther Herskovic
born - England, 1917
died - age 25
     Auschwitz, 1942

Giselle (Katie) Herskovic
born - 1938
died - age, 4 years
     Auschwitz, 1942

Germaine Herskovic
born - 1941
died - age 14 months
     Auschwitz, 1942

Leon, Mirele,
friend & Izi
Antwerp,
1942

Madeleine
Antwerp, 1941

Mirele and Izi

Farm in France, Spring 1940

(top row left to right)Farmer's
daughter, Grandmother, farmer
and wife, Armand, Benny
(front row) Mirele,
Esther with baby Katie,
Mirele's brother Itzhak

Mirele, farmer's wife,
Armand, Itzhak
and Benny

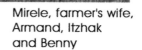

Farmer's wife, Souria & Mirele (16 yrs old)

Madame De Groote, Georges' daughter,
Gaby (his wife after the war),
and Georges

Esther
&
Willy

Willy, Esther, Katie & Germaine
Antwerp, 1941

Mirele and Izi
Antwerp, 1942

Summer 1942

Auntie Riva
with baby Samy,
Morrocan refugee
camp

Grandmother
in front of
Abram's Rue
Des Echelles
apartment,
Brussels

Georges De Groote in
Belgian Police uniform
Antwerp

Mirele,
Brussels
while in hiding

Gestapo
"Studio Willy"
Requisition Order
Signed, Dr.Wilhem Neher
dated, June 1, 1942

(original in U.S. Holocaust
Museum, Washington, DC)

Der Militärbefehlshaber
in Belgien und Nordfrankreich
Militärverwaltungschef

Gruppe : XII – Az. P/W/GA 21 s.
L·34·1187

An die Firma *William Herskovic*

Handelsregister Nr. *45253*

Ort : *Antwerpen*

Strasse und Hausnummer *Berlietstraat*

b)Hierbij wordt U op grond van § 17 der verordening van 31 mei 1941 van den Militairen Bevelhebber in België en Noord-Frankrijk, houdende ekonomische maatregelen tegen de Joden (Derde
Jodenverordening), te rekenen van *1·6·42* de voortzetting van Uw bedrijf, dat
onder het in het adres opgegeven nummer in het handelsregister is ingeschreven, ontzegd. Van
dit tijdstip af is het U verboden zoowel Uw bedrijf voort te zetten, alsook iedere andere zelfstan-
dige werkzaamheid in het bedrijfsleven uit te oefenen.

Uw bedrijfsvermogen moet, met uitzondering van het eventueel daartoe behoorende bezit aan
onroerende goederen, uiterlijk *31·5·42* gelikwideerd en de schrapping van Uw firma
in het handelsregister uiterlijk dit datum aangevraagd zijn. Indien gij een vergunning om te
venten en te leuren (leurderskaart) bezit, afgeleverd op grond van het besluit van 28 November
1930, zoo moet deze onverwijld bij den bevoegden dienst van het Belgisch Ministerie van
Ekonomische Zaken, Wetstraat, 43 te Brussel, worden ingeleverd. Bezit aan onroerende goederen, dat deel uitmaakt van Uw bedrijfsvermogen moet uiterlijk *1·5·42* bij de Afde-
ling Ekonomie van den Chef van het Militair Bestuur, Groep XII, Cantersteen, 47, te Brussel
worden aangegeven. Ten aanzien van de likwideering van het bezit aan onroerende goederen
zullen nog bijzondere aanwijzingen worden gegeven.

De Heer *Dr. Wilhelm Neher* is met ingang van *10·V·42* op grond
van de Derde Jodenverordening van 31 Mei 1941 tot beheerder benoemd, en is als zoodanig met
de uitvoering van en het toezicht op de likwideering van Uw onderneming belast. Uw aandacht
wordt nadrukkelijk gevestigd, op het feit dat alle rechten van Uw
onderneming te leiden en te vertegenwoordigen, alsook van een raad van bestuur, van een raad
van beheer en van de algemeene vergadering rusten voor den duur van het beheer. De rechten
van al deze personen en lichamen worden voor den duur van het beheer uitsluitend uitgeoefend
door den Heer *Dr. Wilhelm Neher* wiens aanwijzingen stipt moeten worden nageleefd.

Ten aanzien van kosten en rechten van beheer zullen nog nadere aanwijzingen worden gegeven.

Met nadruk wordt verwezen naar de strafbepalingen onder § 24 der verordening van 31 Mei 1941
van den Militairen Bevelhebber in België en Noord-Frankrijk, ter zake van handelingen in strijd
met deze voorschriften begaan.

---

a Belgien und Nordfrankreich
Militärverwaltungschef
Gruppe : XII Az. P/W GA 21 s

Auf Grund von § 17 der Verordnung des Herrn Militärbefehlshabers in Belgien und
Nordfrankreich über wirtschaftliche Massnahmen gegen Juden (Dritte Judenverordnung) vom
31.5.1941 wird Ihnen hierdurch die Fortführung Ihres Geschäftsbetriebes unter der in der
Anschrift angegebenen Handelsregisternummer mit Wirkung vom *1·6·42* ab
untersagt. Von diesem Zeitpunkt ab ist Ihnen sowohl die Fortsetzung Ihres Geschäftsbetriebes
als auch jede andere selbständige wirtschaftliche Betätigung verboten.

Ihr Geschäftsvermögen mit Ausnahme des dazu gegebenenfalls gehörenden Grundbesitzes
ist bis zum *31·5·42* zu liquidieren und die Löschung Ihrer Firma im Handelsregister
bis zu diesem Zeitpunkt zu beantragen. Sofern Sie im Besitz einer Genehmigung für den
ambulanten Handel (carte d'ambulant) auf Grund der Verordnung vom 28.11.1930 sind, ist
diese unverzüglich an die Dienststelle des belgischen Wirtschaftsministeriums, Brüssel, rue
de la Loi, 43, abzugeben. Zum Geschäftsvermögen gehörender Grundbesitz ist bis
zum *1·5·42* an die Wirtschaftsabteilung des Militärverwaltungschefs, Gruppe XII,
Brüssel, Cantersteen, 47, zu melden. Ueber die Liquidierung des Grundbesitzes ergehen
noch besondere Anordnungen.

Zur Durchführung und Ueberwachung der Liquidation Ihres Unternehmens ist Herr
Dr. Wilhelm Neher mit Wirkung vom *10·V·42* als Verwalter aufgrund der 3. Judenverordnung vom 31.5.1941 eingesetzt worden. Es wird ausdrücklich darauf hingewiesen, dass während
der Dauer der Verwaltung sämtliche Rechte der zur Leitung und Vertretung Ihres Unternehmens berechtigten Personen sowie eines etwa vorhandenen Vorstandes, Aufsichtsrates
und der Generalversammlung ruhen. Die Rechte aller dieser Personen und Organe werden
während der Dauer der Verwaltung ausschliesslich von Herrn *Dr. Wilhelm Neher*
ausgeübt, deren Anweisungen unbedingt Folge zu leisten ist. *Dr. WILHELM*
Wegen der Kosten und Gebühren für die Verwaltung ergeht besondere Anordnung.

Auf die strafbestimmungen in § 24 der Verordnung des Herrn Militärbefehlshabers in
Belgien und Nordfrankreich vom 31.5.1941 bei Zuwiderhandlungen wird ausdrücklich
hingewiesen.

Für den Militärbefehlshaber
in Belgien und Nordfrankreich
Der Militärverwaltungschef
I. A.

Übersetzung in
a) französisch;
b) flämisch;

a)En vertu du § 17 de l'ordonnance du 31 mai 1941 de Monsieur le Commandant Militaire pour
la Belgique et le Nord de la France relative aux mesures économiques prises à l'égard des juifs
(3me ordonnance relative aux juifs), il vous est fait défense à partir du *1·6·42* de con-
tinuer l'exercice de votre commerce sous le numéro du registre de commerce, figurant à l'adresse
de votre entreprise commerciale. A partir de cette même date vous est interdite non seulement
la continuation de votre commerce mais encore l'exercice de toute autre occupation économique
indépendante.

Jusqu'au *31·5·42* votre avoir commercial, à l'exception de la propriété immobilière
qui en fait partie, devra être liquidé. A cette même date vous devrez avoir requis la radiation de
votre firme du registre de commerce. Si en vertu de l'arrêté du 28 novembre 1930, vous seriez
en possession d'une carte d'ambulant, vous avez l'obligation de la remettre immédiatement au
service compétent du Ministère belge des Affaires Economiques, Bruxelles, rue de la Loi, 43.
Jusqu'au *1·5·42* vos biens immobiliers faisant partie de votre actif commercial
doivent faire l'objet d'une déclaration à adresser à la section des Affaires Economiques du Chef
de l'Administration Militaire, groupe XII, Bruxelles, Cantersteen, 47. La liquidation de ces biens
immobiliers sera régie par des ordonnances ultérieures.

Pour l'exécution et la surveillance de la liquidation de votre commerce, Monsieur *Dr. Wilhelm
Neher* a été désigné conformément à la Troisième Ordonnance relative aux Juifs
du 31 mai 1941, à titre d'administrateur à partir du *10·V·42*. Votre attention est parti-
culièrement attirée sur le fait que pendant la durée de l'administration, tous les droits des personnes, qualifiées pour la direction et la représentation de votre entreprise ainsi que du conseil
de direction, du conseil d'administration ou de l'assemblée générale seront suspendus.

Tous les droits de ces personnes seront pendant la durée de l'administration exercés exclusive-
ment par Monsieur *Dr. Wilhelm Neher* dont les instructions devront être suivies
méticuleusement. Les frais et les honoraires qui seront occasionnés par cette administration
seront déterminés par une ordonnance spéciale. Votre attention est spécialement attirée sur les
sanctions pénales prévues pour la répression des infractions, par le § 24 de l'ordonnance de
Monsieur le Commandant Militaire pour la Belgique et le Nord de la France.

Convoy No 32,
Date, September 14, 1942

CONVOI N° 32 EN DATE DU 14 SEPTEMBRE 1942

Ce convoi a quitté la gare du Bourget/Drancy,le 14 septembre,avec 1000 Juifs,sous la direction de l'Oberfeldwebel Möller,à destination d'Auschwitz. C'est ce que signale le télex rédigé par le SS Heinrichsohn,signé par son supérieur Röthke. Ce télex est adressé comme les précédents à Eichmann, à l'Inspection des KZ et au commandant d'Auschwitz (XXVb-162).

Du point de vue des nationalités,les Allemands ont répertorié: 447 indéterminés (des déportés,dont les Allemands,dans leur hâte de les faire partir au plus vite,n'ont pas relevé la date et le lieu de naissance,ainsi que la nationalité), 220 Polonais,85 Turcs,73 Hongrois,55 Russes,40 Roumains, 37 Français,19 Allemands,14 Hollandais,8 Yougoslaves,7 Autrichiens,7 apatrides, 6 Tchèques,5 Lithuaniens,4 Belges,2 Slovaques,1 Sarrois,1 Letton.

Cette liste,sur papier pelure,est en très mauvais état; comme pour beaucoup d'autres c'est à la loupe qu'il a fallu déchiffrer de nombreux noms.

Il y a environ 640 hommes et 340 femmes dans ce convoi,où l'on compte plus de 60 enfants (sans oublier ceux qui se trouvent parmi les 220 déportés dont on ignore l'âge).

Cette liste est constituée à l'aide de 7 sous-listes:

1/ "Drancy": Il s'agit surtout de Juifs domiciliés à Paris; 550 hommes et femmes. Les renseignements indiqués sont: noms,prénoms,dates et lieux de naissance,nationalités,professions et adresses.

2/ "partants de dernière heure": il s'agit de 83 personnes,hommes et femmes. Pour la plupart d'entre eux,il n'existe comme renseignement,outre le nom et le prénom,que le camp ou la ville de provenance (Compiègne,La Lande,Poitiers, Nice). Un certain nombre d'enfants se trouve certainement dans cette liste, car on y relève des familles: 4 Freiser,4 Herzkowitz.

3/ "Chalons": 20 personnes de nationalités diverses. Une enfant de 3 ans, Gisèle Blech.

4/ "Toulouse-Montluçon": 140 personnes,parmi lesquelles plusieurs familles, tels les 7 Abisch,dont 3 enfants,Maurice 11,Marie 8,Adèle 5; tels Otto 32 et Suzanne 23 Hauser et leur fillette Myriam 2.

5/ "Compiègne": 133 noms et prénoms sans dates et lieux de naissance. Il s'agit seulement d'hommes adultes.

6/ "La Lande": 57 personnes,parmi lesquelles plusieurs familles: Felix 38 et Marie 33 Batista et leurs 3 enfants,Fanny 10,Charles 6 et Cécile 3; Maza Reiter 39 et ses 4 enfants,Hélène 12,Félicie 10,Jacqueline 8 et Marcel 3.

7/ "Belfort": 25 personnes,dont 8 Hollandais. Parmi eux un bébé d'1 an,Dora Topelberg.

A leur arrivée à Auschwitz,le 16 septembre,furent sélectionnés 58 hommes qui reçurent les matricules 63898 à 63953 et 49 femmes qui reçurent les matricules 19772 à 19820. Le reste du convoi fut immédiatement gazé,à l'exception des hommes qui furent sélectionnés avant l'arrivée à Auschwitz,à Kosel (voir fin de la notice du convoi n° 24). Un de ces survivants,Ernest Nives,qui vit aujourd'hui à New-York,nous a confirmé que,parti par ce convoi, il fut sélectionné avec plus d'une centaine d'hommes valides à Kosel.

En 1945,il y avait à notre connaissance environ 45 survivants de ce convoi.

P	HERMALIN	ANNA	.85	VARSOVIE	P
IND	HERSCENBERG	WOLF	01.10.94	VARSOVIE	P
P	HERSKOP	HETTE	22.05.00	NEUSANDATZ	
HOL	HERSZKOWIER	VEL-KORN	08.06.16	ZIKLIN	
HOL	HERSZLIKOVITZ	JESSON	13.10.97	LODZ	
P	HERZKOWITZ	GERMAINE			
P	HERZKOWITZ	GISELLE			
	HERZKOWITZ	WILLIAM			
	HERZKOWITZ	ESTHER			
H	HEUMANN	FLORA	30.01.91	LAUPHEIM	
	HIGELSKI	SALOMON			
IND	HIRSCH	MARTHE	14.06.03	ROGATEN	
IND	HIRSCH	LEON	23.11.03	ROGATEN	
IND	HIRSCH	JEAN	20.04.31	NEUSTETTIN	
IND	HIRSCHOVA	EDITH	06.06.09	PRAGUE	
R	HIRSON	BEATRICE	06.02.21	BERLIN	TC
	HIRTH	LEON	12.12.02	LOUHA	A
IND	HOCHBAUM	JACOB	10.06.76	VARSOVIE	

though Mirele giggled as any teen might, she would never allow anything more to come of it.

In the late 1960s, some twenty-five years later when I was fourteen, we traveled to Belgium. My family visited a couple and their twenty-year-old daughter. As we had tea in the small apartment, I noticed my mother take off her own gold watch and place it on the young girl's wrist. No words. No fanfare. Simply a gesture. I remember wondering why. Years later I would understand. This was Georges De Groote, his wife Gaby, and their twenty-year-old daughter who, coincidentally, was just one year older than my mother had been when Georges had done so much to help her stay alive.

The autumn months of 1942 passed routinely. My mother's preoccupation was not just with her own survival, but with the desperate desire to keep her parents hidden and fed. Unlike many in hiding, her hours were not spent so much in fear of being apprehended by the Gestapo, but obsessed with how to avoid them on her trips to Antwerp for the ration cards; how to pass as a gentile; how to find food that could be purchased locally, and where to find the cash to do so.

Desperate to earn some money, my mother, Fincha Abrams, Warren's daughter, and his mistress Jeannine frequented the flea markets in search of old, torn wool coats that could be bought for a pittance. They then worked long hours, first tearing the garments to shreds looking for whatever wool was salvageable; then cutting and sewing them into wool mittens. As they entered what would be one of the toughest winters in memory, most winter garments were being sent to German soldiers at the front, so manufacturing inexpensive gloves seemed a good idea.

The sewing machines they used were located in the attic of a

97

nearby brothel owned by none other than Warren. There, the prostitutes quickly became friends with the three young women, and it was there that my innocent mother learned much of the ways of the world.

"Mirele, have you ever been naked in front of that husband of yours?" one asked with a giggle.

"I bet not," smiled another.

"Join us," a third would tease, "you'll make much more money than you will sewing those old nasty gloves."

The hours passed quickly. There in the dusty attic, Mirele, Fincha, and Jeannine were just three women, joking and working their days away. And when the adventure had played itself out, the three enterprising seamstresses had completed over five hundred pairs of woolen mittens without a clue as to how to sell them. My mother had learned from youth that in matters of money, Benny would often come to her aid. But because he had little desire to trade in anything less than a diamond, he quickly pawned the entire inventory at a nearby shop he knew well. Of course, with no intention of ever buying them back. Benny was the ladies' hero. The girls were satisfied with their humble earnings. And the pawnbroker undoubtedly did well in the resale.

One day, as Mirele and Fincha were returning to her grandmother's apartment, Mirele sensed a neighbor looking at her oddly. It was most certainly a time of justifiable paranoia, and the look provided just enough to set Mirele off.

"Did you notice her?" she questioned Fincha. "I'm sure she was staring."

"Don't be silly," Fincha tried to calm her friend.

"I've a feeling they're coming for us...why not; they've taken just about everyone we know," Mirele nervously confided in her friend. "All it takes is one of them...one call to the Gestapo and we're gone. If someone's already called, the Germans could come tonight."

"Stay with me then," Fincha offered quickly. "Your parents too. If you're right, the Gestapo will come and find no one."

So that very evening Mirele and her parents moved from Madame Abrams's small apartment to an even smaller one in a much larger low-income housing building. The first evening, as my grandparents slept in Fincha's bed, Mirele and Fincha lay on the floor trying to fall asleep, when the sound of boots pounding down the halls and up the stairs tore into the quiet. Mirele was sure her fears had come to pass, and that even changing their address hadn't helped, as their time had finally come.

She quickly ran into the small bedroom and woke her parents with anxious and panicked words, "Mama, get dressed... they're here for us... Papa, get up!"

She then immediately ran to the window and threw it open.

"Fincha, you must leave this minute," she begged her friend. "They'll take you, too, when they find us. You're not a Jew. There's no reason to risk it. Please, go," Mirele implored her.

"I won't leave," Fincha stated solidly. "If they take you, then they'll have to take me too. You'll need help caring for your mother. I'll be there to help you."

No matter how my mother beseeched her, she wouldn't budge. And as their whispered argument mounted, they heard the boots pass them and continue up the stairs beyond their floor. Relief was very short-lived, for within seconds, there they were again... bounding down the stairs toward them. The girls' hearts raced as they heard the pounding seemingly approach their door a second time. But, again, the sound of boots passed the door and continued down the stairs and out of the building.

Suddenly, there was a chilling quiet. Fincha snuck into the hall and learned that two underground fighters had been apprehended. When she returned to her apartment, the girls were so aware of the quiet, it was as if nothing had ever happened... as if the SS had never run through the halls outside their door. As if their hearts had never pounded in their chests. Everything seemed to be exactly as it had been just moments earlier, in every way but one — for in those few moments when character is defined, Fincha had proved to have become more of a friend in their short months together than most others after an entire lifetime. And Mirele would never forget it.

Chapter Ten

The Plan — Willy

> "That was the tragedy. Not that one man had the courage to be evil. But that millions had not the courage to be good."
>
> John Fowles, *The Magus*

Endless hours turned to endless days, and then weeks. All that seemed to change was one's own body. First the fat melted away, then came a constant weakening and wasting away of the muscles and sinew that held its frame together. Then, the frame itself weakened as the bones began to deteriorate. And of course, the mind suffered as well. My father had heard about the Rauff truck in his first few days in the camp of death from his co-worker on the railroad ties, the sickly man who chose death on the truck over another day of forced labor. But as Willy's own body began to give way, he chose to forget what he'd been told about the death truck. The guards announced that a truck was coming to take those who were feeling weak to a camp where the work would be less taxing.

"All men needing easier work should line up," they called out.

The absurdity was ignored. Willy was so exhausted and starved that he wanted to believe that there was another camp with easier labor, and so he lined up with some thirty others who felt they couldn't take another day. Willy was about fifteenth in line as the truck — a large, metal monster — pulled up. The men at the front of the line began to board, and as Willy neared the entrance, the doctor appeared miraculously from his office where he'd left two SS men and a German military doctor. He walked right up to my father.

"Is it true?" Willy asked his friend, "the rumor that you go in with the car and out with smoke.... Is it true?"

"Straight to the crematorium, Willy. One hundred percent," the doctor confirmed. "Each man must sign a paper that says he is untreatable — terminal. Then both I, as a Jewish doctor, and the German officer must also sign," he gestured toward one of the military men awaiting him back at his office. "Willy," he continued firmly, "you *will* be killed."

With this, just before his turn to board, Willy left the line and chose life. An instant — the same strange instant that had kept him from boarding the deadly accident-bound bus in his youth. Had the whites of his eyes not turned black when he was a teen, or had the doctor not come toward him at that very moment in the camps, my father would have surely boarded one of these death trucks. Timing. Luck. A moment of kindness. Funny notions when you're in the abyss. But somehow they found a hidden entrance and brought a light to show him his way.

But, then again, the world inside the camp was always surreal. Some strangely efficient form of group insanity reigned. And all those loyal servants of this insanity would have most certainly been deemed certifiable if checked out by today's psychiatrists. Physical, mental, and medical torture all performed in the name of Hitler — who was nothing more than a short, angry man — and those who executed these horrors were in charge. The prisoners could only stand by in terrified wonderment. The lunatics were most certainly running the asylum.

One day a German officer came to check the barracks. He chose my father to stay behind that day to report to another officer due to arrive from the outside to inspect the camp.

"You are to say everything is fine," he ordered Willy. "You are not to say anything negative or you will be killed when I return. Understand?"

Nodding dutifully, Willy thought he in fact understood perfectly, "You are all insane."

And when the officer came, Willy reported all was fine with the thirty-two men in his barrack. The officer looked around, hands clasped behind his back as he paced the room. He stopped in front of a makeshift wooden cabinet, sloppily constructed from old crates and leaning against one wall.

The officer opened the door and exclaimed, "Look how this looks! You are destroying our furniture! This must be straightened, cleaned and fixed!" he barked.

"Yes," Willy responded numbly, and the officer left. Willy stared at the cabinet — a rickety nothing, which stood inside a barrack where people were being slowly murdered through starvation and any other available form of inhumanity. He wondered where the insanity had started, and even more, where it would stop. Logic, so intrinsic to his personality, was nowhere to be found.

My father often muses at the absurdity of blaming Hitler for everything. Perhaps it was just an easy excuse for the Germans who survived.

"Just following orders," they would say over and over in the trials and confrontations in the years to follow.

But really, how could one man have been responsible for so much evil? Instead, my father contends that the insanity, which spread like a virus, was everywhere, and in almost every one of these men. He recalls a day of hunger when he watched with wide eyes as a young German guard finished an apple in front of him. When the guard tossed the core to the ground, Willy looked on hungrily, planning to quickly retrieve it and savor the small amount of pulp and seeds that the guard had left uneaten.

But the young guard knew this, so when he tossed the apple he waited an instant as if to give false hope, then with the ball of his foot, inside polished black leather boots, he squashed the core down, deep into the mud. There was nothing left to retrieve of it when he'd finished the rite.

Willy would never forget that small act of what he recognized as violence perpetrated directly against him and the others. Odd how war can give even the lowliest soldier the ability to infuse the smallest gesture with sadistic malice equal to pulling the trigger of a gun. Was that Hitler? Or was that one young man caught up in enough hatred to find personal resources of evil to fuel his every action?

When people give up, they begin to die inside. Hitler had promised to annihilate the Jews. Whomever he wouldn't literally murder, he assured would be killed in spirit. And true to his promise, the Nazis were achieving this throughout their camps. Willy and a few acquaintances knew that through inaction they were quickly losing hope, and that they needed to feel that they were fighting back in some small way to regain it. They began to think of what actions they might be able to execute without getting themselves immediately killed. No matter how small the act, they assured themselves, they would be doing *something*, and thereby reaffirming their own existence. Ironically, no matter how insignificant their rebellion, the risks involved certainly included the possibility of death. For example, something as small as a short piece of wire found in a prisoner's possession would be considered "sabotage," and was enough to get him killed. The young prisoners, surrounded by death, were prepared to rebel in any way they could.

One day, while Willy and a few others were working on a truck, they realized that they were able to let out small amounts of gasoline without detection. They did so without ever being caught. And the action, though causing little harm to the Third Reich, was highly significant to the young captives. It represented a line drawn between passive victim and survivor. And crossing that line gave them the strength needed to go on.

Another enemy of hope lay in the fact that the world inside the camp was so isolated, and the prisoners felt completely out of touch with the world outside. And then, for what my father remembers as one short week, hope was given an ally when an English POW camp was set up right next to the labor camp. These new prisoners fueled the spirit of the demoralized Jewish civilian prisoners in my father's camp, who watched the newcomers with utmost interest. After all, these British POWs worked with the pushcarts as did their civilian counterparts, but their style was inspiringly different.

Each morning several of the POWs would intentionally throw over their first few carts, making it impossible for work to continue. In fact, work was put to a dead stop for some time until the situation was righted. The German foremen, military guards, would start to yell — just as they did at the civilians next door in my father's camp. But in the POW camp, the prisoners would yell right back at them. These Allied soldiers, although prisoners, no doubt felt empowered by the fact that they were trained and sent to fight this enemy, and more so, by the fact that they were somewhat protected by the international rules of war. Additionally, the Germans looked upon the POWs as fellow soldiers, affording them a certain respect and a modicum of leniency, whereas these Nazi guards had been taught over many years to look upon the Jews as subhuman. My father and his fellow prisoners looked upon the POWs' behavior with deep satisfaction. They knew that they themselves would be killed for far less disobedience, and it infused them with optimism to see others being able to fight back on somewhat more level ground.

One day during this short week, as he worked in the yard, my father noticed a POW wink at him. The stranger was holding something in his hand. Willy watched cautiously as the man leaned against the fence and pushed it under and into the mud before quickly walking away. Willy knew that if he were noticed going for this treasure, no matter how small, he would surely be beaten. So he waited. He waited as time stood still, until he was sure the guards were busy with something else... and slowly he worked his shovel into the ground moving his "work" ever closer to the fence. Finally, when he was close enough to reach down, he found what the POW had left him — a candy bar with a Red Cross wrapper. As happy as he was that day for the kindness of the young man, a strange anger filled him. He and his fellow "labor death camp" prisoners were dying of starvation by the thousands — yet the Red Cross was blithely able to provide candy bars for Allied POWs.

Within a few months, with the onset of winter and the steady dwindling of my father's weight and strength, his plans for escape began to take shape.

He had long since chosen his team. Leopold Goldwurm was an obvious partner. The blue-eyed electrician, whom my father had known in Belgium, might be able to pass as an Aryan, especially since he didn't have an Eastern European accent. More importantly, he had a cache of small diamonds that would aid in their travels, and his gentile wife back home could perhaps help them when they returned. Told of the plan, twenty-five-year old Goldwurm agreed without a second thought.

My father then approached Joseph Givertz, another man he'd known in Belgium. Originally from Cologne, Joseph and his gentile wife, Margaretha Diedrighs, had fled Nazi Germany in 1932 to come to Antwerp. Years later, when Germany occupied Belgium, an edict was issued that required all German gentiles to return immediately to the *Vaterland* (fatherland), leaving behind their Jewish husbands or wives. Margaretha had left her husband and returned to Cologne. She, like many others, was terrified and felt she had no choice.

Knowing that Cologne was on the Belgian border, Willy thought that she might be able to help hide them and thus give them some time to find a safe crossing point. There was also the advantage of Joseph's perfect Cologne German accent, as recognizable in Europe as a Texan accent is to Americans. Like Leopold, the thirty-six-year-old Joseph quickly agreed.

The third man whom my father approached was from Vienna, where he had been captain of the Viennese Maccabi soccer team before the war. Since money was a crucial element in any escape plan, Willy had chosen him because he knew that, besides having a perfect German accent, and being one of the physically strongest in the camp, this man had American dollars sewn into his coat lining. The young sports star was quick to commit himself to the escape attempt.

Leopold and my father were in the same barracks, but the others lived elsewhere in the camp and had never met. My father, the only link between the three men, would go to see each of them every day in order to make certain his plan would remain alive, as well as secret. Each day, my father would put on three shirts, thinking that we would need them if that day were to become "the" day. And each day was looked upon as a possible opportunity, analyzed but then discarded for one reason or another.

Joseph had been an auto mechanic before the war, and was given that same job in the camp. My father knew that when the time was right they would have to cut through the barbed-wire fence, which, fortunately, unlike other camps, was not electrified. Figuring Joseph had the best access to the proper tool, he instructed him to find a wire-cutter. Joseph showed up a day later with a shockingly conspicuous two-foot-long appliance. My father took the cutter and quickly buried it in a pile of snow that bordered his barrack. He knew there would be snow to keep it hidden for at least six months, and that if they had not escaped by then, there wouldn't be enough left of their bodies or souls to do so.

Willy constantly studied the camp's perimeter. He found the one spot that seemed perfect. Ironically, a week before the eventual escape, he and two others were ordered to reinforce that very spot.

Willy sold the boots he'd once hidden in his coat sleeves. The Polish worker that acquired them gave him enough German marks to enable the eventual purchase of train tickets.

One Saturday, my father told Walde, the contractor, that he was an artist. He told Walde that if he would bring him a photo of a loved one, paper, and three *Kohinoor Hartmoth* charcoals, he would happily draw him a portrait on his day off. Walde was moved by the offer, and promised that he would collect the items over the weekend, and then obtain permission for Willy to work in his office where it would be warm and comfortable. They both knew that time spent in the warm office would be life-saving — a kind offer my father would never forget, though it never actualized because by the time Walde returned with paper, photo, and charcoals, my father was gone.

Chapter Eleven

Mazel — Willy

"We thank You also for the miracles, for the redemption, for the mighty deeds and acts of salvation, wrought by You, as well as for the wars which You waged for our fathers in days of old, at this season. In the days of the Hasmonean, Matityahu son of Yohanan, the High Priest, and his sons, when the iniquitous power of Greece rose up against Your people Israel to make them forgetful of Your Law, and to force them to transgress the statutes of Your will, then did You in your abundant mercy rise up for them in the time of their trouble; You pleaded their cause, You judged their suit, You avenged their wrong, You delivered the strong into the hands of the weak, the many into the hands of the few, the impure into the hands of the pure, the wicked into the hands of the righteous, and the arrogant into the hands of those that occupied themselves with Your Law: for Yourself You made a great and holy name in Your world, and for Your people Israel You worked a great deliverance and redemption as at this day. And thereupon Your children came into the oracle of Your house, cleansed Your temple, purified Your sanctuary, kindled lights in Your holy courts, and appointed these eight days of Hanukkah in order to give thanks and praises unto Your great name."

Al Hanisim prayer (adapted by Chaim Weinreb, Department for Jewish Zionist Education, JAFI)

Peiskretscham, Hanukkah, 1942

It was a Sunday night in December of 1942. The first night of Hanukkah, a centuries-old holiday of miracles. The weather was

109

the worst it had been since Willy had been deported. In fact, it was possibly the worst Willy remembered in his entire life. Snow and hail combined with a ferocious wind to create a level of noise that was beyond belief as it screamed between the barracks of the camp.

One of the German guards opened the door to an office and a loud commotion spilled out into the night. Willy noticed that the guard closed the door and went to get more guards. The office in question was filled with the camp's Jewish Kapos, who had decided to throw themselves a Hanukkah celebration. But when the SS guard returned with backup, it was with a vengeance. Willy was certain their screaming and violent beatings were loud enough to be heard for miles.

"You Jewish bastards, you think this is a holiday?!" the Germans yelled at the tops of their lungs.

The batons flew, and the Kapos cried out in pain.

"What do you think you're doing?!" the guards screamed.

"Who do you think you are?!"

"How dare you?!"

"Schweine."

Within moments, somehow every Jew from every barrack was outside trying to hear what was going on. The Kapos had earned the reputation of abusing their fellow Jews and had been a source of great emotional, as well as physical, pain to all the prisoners. Much worse than being tortured by a German, was being tortured and bullied by one of your own — and that was the Kapos' job. So, sadly, along with the fascination of seeing the German guards attack these men, there was an empty and painful satisfaction.

The camp had two watchtowers, each with its own large spotlight. Because of the fracas, the strong beams of light that continually circled the perimeter were both directed to this one

110

area. There were always two surveillance guards on sentry duty — one on the inside of the fence, and one on the outside. They would walk along the encampment fence in opposite directions, crossing each other twice a rotation. But this evening, even these guards left their posts and joined the others.

My father watched it all with rapt attention. It was now or never. There could never be another opportunity like this one. The altercation had in fact eliminated almost every impediment to escape. And the storm was so loud that Willy was certain no one would hear them cutting the wire fence, a sound that would surely have rung out as it carried through the metal chain links under any other circumstance. And though the mud and slush beneath his feet should have slowed him, he moved like the lightning that was filling the sky above, going to each of his partners with one word.

"Now."

Without delay, Willy approached the snow mound that had protected the wire-cutters for over a month. One of the men from his barrack looked suspiciously at the only person coming toward the bunks, while all others scampered in the direction of the fight.

"You're escaping, aren't you?" he looked at Willy pleadingly. "Please take me."

"Don't be ridiculous," Willy painfully denied the man's request.

Too many lives were now at stake, and their plan was far too advanced. He didn't feel he had the right to allow any change that could possibly endanger them all.

"Where would we go on a night like this?" he continued. "We'd never survive."

As he spoke the words that convinced the man there would be no escape, he worked hard to convince himself that the words

111

were not true. The storm, he had to believe, was their visa, and they would survive.

When Willy was safely alone, he dug out the cutters. The weather and amount of time they'd been hidden would have normally made their retrieval difficult, but Willy's strength seemed to be increasing with each handful of snow and mud he scooped away. When he had the tool in hand, he ran to join his waiting friends. He gave the cutters to Joseph, and the other three of them kept watch while he expertly cut a "U" shape into the fence approximately three feet square. He then folded the metal flap upwards, and the four men crawled through. Suddenly the Viennese athlete panicked and ran back into the camp. Willy chased after him, begging him not to give up. Persuaded, the youth followed Willy out of the fence a second time, but once again, he panicked and returned. The three men feared they had no choice but to keep góing and leave the young man behind.

The man's fear was well founded. During their short time at the camp they had seen many failed escapes. Each time, the escapees were brought back to the camp, sometimes after only an hour, sometimes not for days. But whatever the case, they were then killed defenselessly in front of my father and the other fellow prisoners, beaten to death as all were forced to stand by and watch. Death by beating was a ritual that became so common it seemed just a usual end to an average workday. After being beaten to within an inch of their lives, the man would be taken to the doctor, where that last inch would be dealt with.

"When they are brought to me," the doctor had once told Willy, "if they don't die right away, the guards force me to kill them by injection. You see, the tortured are obviously now too weak to serve the German cause." After a long pause, he continued, "I tell myself I'm doing them a favor; putting an end

112

to their nightmare.... But I suppose that is where my own nightmare begins."

There had been one instance, when visiting the doctor's quarters, that my father recognized a young man who'd been beaten to a pulp. His name was Tolkofsky, the son of a *diamondtiere* (diamond merchant) from Antwerp.

"I know this boy," Willy told the doctor. "You cannot inject him."

"He won't eat. He won't even swallow the medication. He'll never survive."

"Please let me help," my father begged. "If I can get him to take the medication...."

"It's no use," the doctor cut him off.

"Please."

"Fine," the doctor acquiesced. "Try then. Be my guest."

Permission granted, Willy held the youth in his arms. Tolkofsky was black and blue from head to toe. His eyes and body were swollen almost beyond recognition. My father tried to give him medication. Holding the boy tight, he tried over and over again, but the medication wouldn't go down. It poured from the boy's mouth all over Willy's clothing, but he continued to try nonetheless.

"Willy, you see it is of no use," the doctor explained as a matter of fact. "His insides are as swollen as his outside. Everything in him is swollen shut."

At that time, word had filtered into the camp of some Soviet advances against the German and Italian forces in Russia. So Willy spoke to the dying boy in his arms, trying to infuse some hope that might save the young man's life.

"It is only a matter of time," he told young Tolkofsky. "Soon we will be liberated, and you will be in your own mama's arms before you know it."

Willy knew the young man had heard him, because with no fight left nor the strength to speak, with his last breath barely heard, he sounded out one word as he died in my father's arms.

"Mama," he sighed.

Having seen firsthand what the Germans did to those that tried to escape, my father didn't blame the young athlete from Vienna for running back. At least in the camps they knew what to expect — outside the barbed wire, all bets were off.

The map that had been drawn in the snow for my father by the Polish carpenter depicted a small village nearby. So, sans their fourth companion, Willy, Joseph, and Leopold headed in that direction. But, of course, the same conditions that made the escape possible, now made the journey treacherous. The night was so black they couldn't even see one another as they ran. And because they certainly couldn't see more than a meter in any direction, they were stunned when they found themselves bathed in an eerie blue light that emanated from a small police station that appeared to suddenly manifest directly in front of them.

They immediately noticed a guard at its front door, who fortunately didn't notice them. Quickly crossing the street, they came to a wooden fence more than seven feet high. Leopold jumped up and climbed over first. Then my father. Even though he'd felt weakened for so long, with his weight having dropped from one-seventy to just over a hundred pounds, out of some strange reserve came the ability to leap the fence as if he was flying. The fact that they had been starving for months seemed irrelevant as adrenalin poured into their systems, fueling them like a drug.

The three fugitives soon found themselves in a village, terrified of being seen. So, despite the blinding weather conditions, they began to run along the fields off the main road, which almost assured the possibility of getting lost. Dogs were barking in every direction as the men ran through each village and headed toward the next. All the while their heads raced.

"When will they realize we're gone?"

"Have they already?!"

"Has their search for us begun?"

"If not, when will it?"

"How will they chase us?"

"How many will there be?"

The escapees had now covered so much distance so quickly, they knew the guards would never find them if they, too, were on foot. Fearing they'd veer off course and lose their way, they decided to continue alongside the road. They surmised that if a search would be made by car, the lights would warn them to hide long before they'd be detected in this storm. That seemed to afford less risk than the uncertainty of going through the fields. But, always concerned that their captors might come up on them from behind, they were shocked when a flashlight blinded them from ahead. Holding it, they discerned, were three German officers who stood before them in the rain. The fugitives felt their hearts firmly lock into their throats.

"*Guten Abend.* There is a bar nearby. Where is it?" the officers asked.

"Two kilometers back, that way. There," revealing none of his fear, Joseph responded without the slightest pause, gesturing the direction from which they'd run. "Turn right, and it is on your left. You cannot miss it."

As the contented officers continued on their way toward the fictitious bar, and the fugitives' heartbeats began to return to normal, they looked at one another and realized that had the flashlight illuminated my father's coat, all would have been over. Most in their camp, where no uniform was provided, were forced to paint stars on their clothing, as the guards looked on. Willy and his partners, in anticipation of their escape, had sewn theirs on so that they could simply tear them off as soon as they were outside the camp. But what they now realized in the dimmest of light was that Willy's had only partially come off. Tearing off the last remnant and the labor camp it had now come to represent, a realization overtook him — after all the events that he had experienced, in which God and / or luck had coldly left him, God suddenly seemed to be on his side. Something had definitely shifted from those early nightmare days where everything that could have gone wrong, did. For now, the guardian angel of his youth seemed to have finally found him in his darkest hour, and joined him for his journey home.

The plan had been to take a train. The closest station being forty kilometers away, they ran for what seemed an eternity. Willy, overtaken by some strange inner momentum powered only by will, seemed always in the lead, stopping regularly to wait for the other two. He wondered at this strength with no idea where it could possibly be coming from. His skin hung on his long, lanky bones as if there were nothing else in him. But it was there. Somewhere he had stored whatever it was he needed to successfully accomplish life.

And they ran.

Hours passed... and they kept running.

They ran alongside the road until lights would warn of potential danger. Then they'd run as far from the road as possible without losing sight of it. Once. Twice. The third time, they found themselves face to face with barbed wire. They climbed up and over the top, and then with absolutely no visibility of what lay beyond, they had no choice but to jump.

116

They found themselves falling into a deep ravine. The barbed wire had obviously been placed there to protect people from such a fall. The depth of this ravine, augmented by the ice and snow, made getting out nearly impossible. But after a relentless struggle, they succeeded.

And the running began anew.

Again, lights.

And again, they were forced to leave the safety of the road, this time running into the woods. Still blinded by the storm, Willy found himself running full speed into a tree. His front tooth broke from the impact, and though there wasn't even an instant to worry about it, it would remain a lifelong reminder of his flight that night.

Maybe it was the shock of the collision, but as suddenly as his energy had manifested, after having run relentlessly for over four hours, it now dissipated. They were deep in the snow-covered forest at around midnight when Willy said that he had to stop, to regenerate. He fell asleep immediately beside a tree, sinking into the thick blanket of snow that covered the ground around them. He was so exhausted that his body never even felt the cold and the warning it offered. Knowing the danger of his freezing to death, Joseph and Leopold woke him. But his exhaustion was so great that he fell asleep again, and then again. Thankfully, they were there to wake him each time. There is no question that had he been alone that night, he would never have made it out of the freezing forest alive.

Miraculously recharged after thirty minutes, they were back on the run. And oddly, once again Willy found himself running faster than the others, waiting or doubling back at regular intervals. Eventually they saw the lights of a nearby village. It seemed to be only three hundred meters away when Willy's legs began to give out; they refused to listen to his brain's commands.

The will was there, but suddenly, that was all there was. So with his legs no longer listening, Willy had to use his hands and arms. As if they were no longer a part of his body, he grabbed his legs one at a time, literally lifting and placing each one step forward.

When the men finally reached the station, they realized that, having left the road, they had missed the first town and had actually traveled eight kikometers further than they'd planned. Learning that the next train was to arrive in an hour, Joseph took the cash that Willy had procured back at the camp and bought three tickets to Breslau. It was the closest large city, and they knew that the larger the city, the greater chance of anonymity.

They waited quietly in the small village station. Because the Germans had requisitioned so much civilian labor, the three — surprisingly — did not stand out. Like the workers in the station, they were tanned and dirty. And even though Willy was emaciated, having been in the camps the longest, one might have been fooled by his three layers of clothing and hands so dirty and swollen, they were twice their normal size.

They watched a large clock mounted above the ticket window. The men were so anxious that the hands seemed to barely move. Time in fact stood still, but their fatigue and hunger were relentless, a condition exacerbated by the appearance of a woman who entered the station and sat down on the bench directly in front of them. In her lap was a freshly baked bread. It was enormous, either in actuality or as a result of their desire for it. The men couldn't take their eyes off it, each craving it more than they'd remembered ever craving anything in their lives. But they didn't dare make a move or say a word. They knew their lives might actually depend upon their silence.

When an eternity had passed, the train finally rolled into the small station and the three men quietly boarded.

Chapter Twelve

One Day to the Next — Mirele

Brussels, Winter, 1942

The days in hiding passed from one to the next. The fear of going into the streets was ever present, yet somehow forgotten. Mirele found herself adapting quite well, though a side glance from a German soldier or the sound of a black Citroën screeching up to the curb could send her stomach promptly into her throat. The days were spent in her new friendship with Fincha, her trips with De Groote to the ration card office, worrying about the state of her young husband, and of course, about money.

True to form, her brother made frequent stops at the apartment, and more often than not, brought cash. Mirele also became friends with a young woman named Jacqueline who owned a local pub. Once a week Mirele would earn a few francs by doing the woman's hair. The job was always pleasant, as Jacqueline was full of stories that made my mother laugh. Apparently, Jacqueline enjoyed a certain promiscuity, the memories of which she gladly shared with her young hairdresser. There was an escape into the humor of these experiences that allowed Mirele to hold on to the normality within the insanity, while of course making a bit of cash at the same time.

Whenever she accumulated a few francs from her work or her brother's benevolence, she would quickly run to a nearby vendor where she would purchase just about the only item that wasn't rationed — the abundant local tiny fish. Always thrilled with the acquisition, she would run them home to her mother, who would quickly turn them into a delicious treat.

Chapter Thirteen

The Miraculous Journey — Willy

Breslau, Germany, the First Day of Hanukkah, 1942

The train ride for Willy, Joseph, and Leopold came to an uneventful end as the train entered the Breslau station. They were certain that their luck on that first night of Hanukkah had been more than an immeasurable gift — in fact, a miracle befitting the holiday. Still, they couldn't help wondering how long it would last. Knowing that all the train stations were filled with Gestapo, each man found his heart pounding in his chest. Quickly noticing two exits, and without the luxury of conversation or detailed planning, they split up to avoid suspicion.

Willy intentionally found his way into the middle of a mass of more than a hundred people exiting the station. Hoping to become invisible, he remained at the core of the group as they all funneled through a small exit. Suddenly, he spotted a guard staring straight at him. A split second passed between this eye contact and the guard's command.

"You. Stop," he ordered.

But he was too late. My father, anticipating the command, used that very split second to slide out of the station, and out of sight.

Less than a moment. Another "lucky" moment.

It was around nine o'clock in the morning as my father's feet hit the sidewalk outside the station and he found himself bathed in the bright light that shines on cold, crisp winter days. He felt the wind on his face, and the warmth that the sun manages to deliver even on the coldest of days following a storm. And then it came — the sudden realization that he was finally free. Even with all the impending danger and the painful losses that he would be left to deal with for a lifetime, he felt total elation. It overwhelmed him as nothing had ever done before, but the sense of joy was short-lived. The peril quickly came back into focus when he noticed Joseph up ahead. Standing behind him in the light for the first time, Willy was shocked to see the shape of the Star of David clearly in the otherwise faded fabric of Joseph's coat. Although they had ripped off the star patch, its memory had been left behind from the months of working outdoors in the sun, much like a wall's memory of a painting that is taken down after having hung in a certain spot for years.

Willy quickly approached Joseph, stooping to grab a chunk of dirt from the ground as he walked. Calling out a greeting to his unsuspecting friend, Willy slapped the dirt all over his back, obliterating the faded image of the star.

Leopold soon approached the two, and, as if guided by radar, they all spotted a small restaurant across the street. Their eyes went directly to the door, and their feet followed fearlessly.

A heavy woman in her forties stood behind the counter. The young men seated themselves at a small table, knowing they had only a few marks left. Even worse, they were well aware that, with the war, foods were rationed, and they had no ration cards.

"We are mechanics from Cologne," Joseph told the woman, "here to help set up a factory, and have forgotten our ration cards. Could we buy some food without them?"

"I can sell you only the herring salad."

The woman gestured to a large bowl behind her. As in Brussels, small local fish were abundant and therefore available without ration cards.

"Good," Joseph responded. "Three then, *bitte* (please)."

She gave the men three large plates of the seafood concoction, and within seconds it was "inhaled" — disappearing from their plates as if it had never been there. Then, as the three were trying to figure out whether or not they had enough money to order more, Joseph's stomach impatiently spoke out.

"A second, please," the starved young man blurted without further delay.

Leopold and Willy looked at him nervously, knowing payment would be impossible. But before they could say anything, the proprietress, choosing not to question the speed with which they'd eaten, quickly gave them each another portion of salad. This time, even though they'd not ordered them, she added a tall beer and a couple of cigarettes — priceless commodities at the time.

Did she know they were Jews escaped from the nearby camps? Or, did she think they were simply hard-working but poor laborers? The men would never know, but would remain eternally grateful nevertheless, because when they finished their meal and were given the check, they put all the money they had onto her counter, knowing they were extremely short. She took their meager marks without complaint nor a call to the local police — which would most certainly have been a death sentence.

The men had hoped that in a city as large as Breslau there might still be a rabbi. They felt certain that if they could locate him, they would most assuredly find both assistance and information. Unfortunately, they had no idea where to begin their search. Then suddenly, a "guiding light" appeared before them — a young man with the Star of David fastened to his arm.

"Where can we find a rabbi?" the fugitives asked quietly in Yiddish, so that he would not fear their motives.

The young man gave them directions to the only rabbi he knew of nearby. Willy and the two others quickly followed the young Jew's directions. The journey ended with a long flight of stairs leading up to a door that they anxiously knocked on. The door opened and they found themselves standing before a very stoic and elegant German rabbi who invited them in. The room was quite large and had five desks with people working diligently at each. The fugitives began to tell the rabbi of their escape. They tried to talk to him — to tell him of the conditions in the camps, but he didn't want to hear a word.

"Get out of here!" the rabbi suddenly stood and yelled.

It was as if he had no heart, and still today, my father hopes that, in his particular case, it was simply fear.

"Perhaps just some shelter for a night?" Willy questioned.

"You must get out," he continued to yell, immediately opening the door. "This house is under the Gestapo! You're endangering us all. Out. All of you, now!"

Willy, Joseph and Leopold left disheartened beyond words.

"How could this possibly happen in the home of a rabbi?" If they couldn't turn to him, if he wouldn't help them, who would?

Despondent, they slowly descended the stairs of his building. Terrified of making their next move, they were surprised by a young teenage woman who bounded into their path. And, as though some strange spell had been cast upon all three men, they looked at the young stranger, each on his own, certain that they had known her from their past. Though, in reality, none had ever set eyes on her before, this bizarre recognition gave them the full courage to approach her with their story.

"This rabbi has been horrible," she responded with frustration. "He hasn't helped a soul."

She turned back down the stairs.

"Follow me," she calmly instructed.

And they did.

"Behind here. Wait," she gestured to a large door at the bottom of the stairs. "And don't make a sound."

The girl disappeared as quickly as she had appeared, and the men stood there obediently, wondering, after all they'd been through, why they would trust a young girl, not much more than a child, with their safety?

They pondered their situation until she returned with a bag of "gold" in the form of small, hard rolls. As she spoke, the men inhaled the rolls as they had the herring salad just a half-hour before.

"You know, we Jews were thirty-two thousand here in Breslau before the war. Now only six hundred married couples remain here, manufacturing uniforms for the German military. We were the only ones allowed to stay. The others were all deported. I can take only one of you into our home. But I will find friends to take the other two."

And the angel continued, telling them of the world they'd been missing as she guided them to her home. My father stayed with her that night. She placed one of the other two men with a friend, and hid the second in the mortuary of a nearby synagogue.

When she returned that evening, Willy asked, "May I perhaps bathe?"

"I'm afraid for us Jews, there is gas to heat the water only one hour per day," she apologized. "It will be unbearably cold."

All the unbearable things he'd survived during the last months flashed through Willy's mind like a surreal film. *The filth, the pain...*

"The cold water will be fine," he smiled weakly, cutting off his thoughts. He assured her the meager facilities were all a luxury compared to where he'd been.

125

The young girl showed him to the bath and left him to his privacy. It was the second night of Hanukkah and the miracles continued. One day before, he'd been a prisoner in a death-filled labor camp and now he was in the sanctuary of a Jewish home. There, in the solitary darkness of the small room, Willy began to undress completely for the first time in months, and when he caught a glimpse of his image in the mirror, terror coursed through his veins.

"I am nothing but bones," he thought with horror. "The skin merely hangs upon them with nothing between."

If he hadn't realized it sooner, he now was most certain that it was wondrous that he had survived the escape — the storm, the cold, the endless running through the night. A well-fed, strong and healthy man would have had trouble succeeding, let alone the walking corpse he'd become.

He gradually lowered himself into the bath. It was deep into winter. December in Breslau. And without heated water, the bath must certainly have been ice cold, but it felt so good to be bathing that he didn't even notice the chill.

Later during the night, as he tried to sleep, he suddenly found himself soaking wet, submerged in a pool of his own sweat. Oddly, when morning arrived my father emerged a new person. He did not even recognize himself as the young man he was before the war; that youth had died in the camps. Nor even the man he'd seen in the mirror the night before. Instead, as if somehow purged, he'd awoken as a phoenix rising from the ashes of all he'd held dear, someone totally new, and oddly, with the strength of a giant. Survival was no longer a problem, but a path. The only question was where the journey would take him.

The young woman brought the other two men back to her home that morning and they all ate breakfast together. The three men told her their story in detail, waterfalls of words that had no end. They then outlined their plan to return to Belgium.

"You must be crazy," she said, almost laughing at the tragic absurdity of the idea. She explained that no one was moving around Europe successfully these days, and that crossing borders was absolutely impossible.

"Two girls I know studied French for six months. Six months," she added for emphasis. "Spoke it perfectly. Do you believe it? They were to go to Switzerland with false papers and everything," she explained. "They were caught on the train within hours. Just hours! Wouldn't we all escape if we thought we could?"

But the three men were not deterred by her words. Maybe it was false hope — a delusion brought on by the impossible success they'd achieved so far. Maybe it was desperation after the rabbi's rejection. Where would they be safe if not with their own?

That day the three men ventured outside her apartment with the stars sewn back onto their clothing at their rescuer's insistence.

"You'll be much safer this way," she assured.

Within moments on the street, a young German pilot with a woman on his arm noticed the three. He laughed as he gestured toward the yellow stars on their clothes.

"Do you see their new uniform decorations?"

She joined him in his ridicule, and as the fugitives rounded the corner, echoes of laughter refusing to disappear, the three men tore the stars from their clothing, certain they were safer without the label.

All three were positive their chances for surviving the journey back to Belgium would be greatly improved if they could secure the furlough papers that gentile workers were given as weekend passes home. They also knew that they would need money to purchase these, as well as anything else required for their travels. My father still had his large diamond, and later that evening asked their young savior for help in selling it. She quickly contacted someone in Berlin who she knew was buying diamonds. He agreed to come to Breslau immediately.

Willy met with the man and watched him study the stone through a jeweler's loupe.

"How much do you want?" he questioned. "It is full of blemishes. Coal spots," he said, without looking up from the stone.

My father knew diamonds and had the studied, precise eye of an artist. As far as he was concerned, his stone was clean and a perfect blue-white. But as my father began to negotiate, the buyer slyly pulled out letters of recommendation from top German officers with whom he'd apparently traded. It quickly became quite clear who had the best bargaining position. Regardless, in the spirit of negotiation, Willy drove the man up a bit and a deal was struck.

Lack of identification could prove deadly, so their young angel then took her three fugitives to an automatic photo booth.

"You must have something to show," she insisted.

Then, with photos in hand, she easily procured special permits. Though the passes were simply used to secure discounts on the train, she hoped they would be useful if an emergency situation confronted them.

"Because of the photos, they might help as identification if anyone stops you while you're traveling," she explained hopefully. "At least you will have something to show."

So with renewed energy, train passes as identification, and money in their pockets, the men were ready to leave the known dangers of Breslau for the unknown ones that lay beyond its borders. But before they left the young woman's safety, Willy gave her money for all she'd done, his address in Belgium and thanked her from the bottom of his heart.

Tragically, several months later he would receive a postcard wherein she wrote,

> *We have been taken after all. We are en route*
> *to the camps and have no idea if we will survive.*
> *We hope you did. We will throw this card from*
> *the window and maybe it will find you.*

And so it miraculously had. Willy's heart broke when it arrived. "Angels shouldn't suffer," he thought, "and most certainly not at the hands of the devil."

Willy, Leopold, and Joseph nervously made their way out of Breslau by train and arrived safely in Berlin. They must have most certainly become invisible, for in a time of constant military harassment, they were never once asked to show their bogus identification cards that would have done them absolutely no good.

They believed their first order of business should be to shed their prisoner appearance by getting much-needed haircuts. Upon entering the camps, their heads had all been shaved and the hair had grown awkwardly since. They entered the first barbershop they found and almost passed out. There before them were a dozen German officers. Eight sat in a long row of chairs with barbers working diligently behind them; four sat nearby awaiting their turn. My father and his companions knew that if they had any chance of not being taken back to the camps right then and there, it would only be if they looked as if they belonged. Almost as if they'd planned it, their three right hands raised in unison as they all offered a loud, "*Heil,* Hitler."

They then took their places, nonchalantly sitting beside the waiting officers. When their own turn came, they mounted the barber chairs.

Seeing Willy's short hair, the barber asked, "Officers cut?"

"*Jawohl*," yes, my father answered firmly.

Once outside, with hearts returning to normal rhythms, the young fugitives continued to believe that their best chance of help would be in finding a fellow Jew. But by 1942, there weren't many left in Germany, and those few were usually well hidden. The three walked the streets with this goal for hours. Finally, they found a man in his forties with the once-ubiquitous yellow star on his arm. They told him their story as they had done with the young woman, and also that they were in need of the workers' weekend passes to help them cross back over the border into Belgium, and most pressingly, of a place to spend the night.

The man apologized that he lived in a very elegant part of the city and feared that their safety would be compromised if they stayed with him.

"The Gestapo has emptied all the Jews out of the neighborhood up to our block. We are sure they will come to us in a day, or two at the most. If you are found there, we will all surely be killed," he explained.

But when he looked into their desperate eyes he continued, "Everyone in the building has storage in the basement. That is where you'll be the safest."

They spent only that one night, the third miraculous night of Hanukkah, in his storage area. Heeding the good man's warning, they left at dawn. One would think that as they hid in the cold, dark, damp space that night, they would have been overcome with fear, but somehow fear had disappeared. For, in fact, fear clearly had no place to live, as the determined young men's minds were filled with thoughts of returning home. And all that seemed to pump through their veins was the adrenalin needed to get there.

They had heard that they might find the furlough papers they were searching for at a local pastry shop frequented by Belgian TODT workers based in Berlin. So, the minute they left their basement hiding place, they went to locate the small bakery.

On entering, they were greeted by the owner, a large man. A shop like this one could've been found on almost any street in Europe before the war. But a large portrait of Adolf Hitler hanging ominously behind the counter eliminated any sense of comfort the familiarity of the venue provided. The shop was empty, and knowing that they would have to wait for the Belgian workers to arrive, Willy pulled a few of his newly acquired marks from his pocket and gave them to Joseph, who in his perfect German purchased three pastries from the showcase. It seemed that the three men managed to somehow ingest the cakes almost before their hind-sides managed to hit their seats, and Joseph returned to the counter to purchase three more. And when those too were "inhaled," they returned to the burly proprietor again. And then again. As the hands on the clock beside Hitler's portrait kept turning, the men continued their routine. Their stomachs had no bottom. So, after four hours, with not a single Belgian yet in sight, they had thoroughly emptied the small shop's entire case. The large man eyed his hungry customers suspiciously throughout, regardless of their casual and polite manner, and the fact that they paid him each time they ordered.

"We are Belgian workers," Willy had offered sometime between their second and tenth servings. "We have lost our papers and would like to purchase others," he continued, trying not to sound nervous, his eyes averted the dictator's stare from the portrait hanging in front of him.

"Is there any problem with us being here?" This time Willy mildly gestured to the photograph.

"No. No problem," the large proprietor responded. "I'm

Austrian," he continued, in a tone that seemed to say, "I've no allegiance to the man whose likeness hangs behind me."

Willy looked upon the stranger with enormous fondness, certain the shop owner knew he should have been turning in these unlikely patrons. Amazing how nightmarish circumstance gives opportunity for heroes to shape-shift from the most unlikely and humble origins.

After an eternity, young men in brown uniforms with swastikas emblazoned on their arms finally entered the shop. Cautiously, Willy approached the proprietor again.

"Can we trust them?" my father quietly asked.

The Austrian nodded, "They're just TODT. Those boys are as unhappy wearing those uniforms as we are seeing them."

The TODT were semi-military men assembled from all the German-occupied countries and forced to work in uniform for the Nazi cause at minimal wages. They were mainly manual laborers, who worked with great reluctance.

When Willy informed his fellow travelers that the men weren't a risk, Leopold began to tell the now-familiar fiction to them.

"Anyone have a pass they'd like to sell? My mother in Antwerp is sick. We would like to return immediately. There is no time to secure a furlough."

"I'll sell mine," said one young man as he took out his permit. "I'm sure I can get you the two others by tonight."

After a short negotiation, a deal was struck for the three passes. The uniformed young man was paid half, with a promise of the balance when he brought the passes to a designated restaurant at six o'clock that evening.

The restaurant was a huge meeting spot for these TODT laborers. Willy, Leopold and Joseph made their way through the busy place hearing a cacophony of languages that emanated from each of the numerous tables. They finally seated themselves at an empty table for five. There they remained for the eternity that was in reality only one hour, all the while trying to look casual while staring at the two empty chairs that awaited their rendezvous. But there was no sign of the boy. After an endless passage of time, new customers asked for the empty chairs, and not wanting to raise suspicion through hesitation, the fugitives quickly relinquished them.

Their new table-mates began to talk, and my father immediately realized they were Czechs. And with that comfort, Leopold once again began their tale of an ailing mother. As they chatted, one of the two men silently slid his index finger gently over the old wood tabletop, clearly designing a Star of David. Though all three fugitives saw the gesture, they feigned ignorance, not sure of its implication.

Finally, the Czech worker looked accusingly across the table and stated in a vociferous voice, "If I want to go see my sick mother, I go. Papers or not!"

Whether he was simply expressing resentment of his own subservient position as a Nazi forced laborer, or whether he was expressing his suspicion of the three fugitives who stared back at him in terror will never be known, for suddenly, all eyes in the restaurant were on two German MPs who had aggressively just entered, and fortunately, began searching for fellow German soldiers.

And the hours continued to crawl by.

The Czechs were long gone as the clock struck eleven with still no sign of the boy holding the promised weekend passes — the passes they had grown to believe were their tickets for a safe passage and survival. The restaurant was closing, and aware of the midnight curfew, Willy, Joseph, and Leopold had no choice but to go to the station and attempt the train ride to Cologne. The resolution to chance the journey immediately turned to

133

dread when they arrived at the station to learn their train would not depart for four more hours. Four hours, in the middle of the night, seated in a German railway station. To make matters worse, they saw no other civilians around them. Instead, a sea of German military uniforms — thousands of soldiers of all ranks apparently moving from one German outpost to another.

Willy and his friends settled into the reality of their wait. Since their escape, they had eaten for several days. They had washed, shaved, changed clothing, and were now looking more like the workers they claimed to be, than the fugitives they were. And despite their paranoia, they soon realized they were anonymous in this crowd. Unnoticed and unbothered, hiding in plain sight, they most likely appeared to be Gestapo. Who else would dare remain at a railway station, amidst thousands of soldiers, for hours after curfew? Not the TODT, not the local Jews, and most certainly not escaped labor camp prisoners.

After a while, the men decided they would be less conspicuous if they separated for a time with plans to meet up on the train. They had come to find a certain security in traveling together, so when the train arrived at four as scheduled, they were each shocked to hear the announcement over the loudspeaker: "Four o'clock trains to Cologne boarding in ten minutes; Tracks four and six."

"Four and six!" they all panicked. Confusion ran through them. Which train should they board? Would they find one another? They each searched the masses of men milling about the station for sight of the others.

"All aboard!" The words ran with a shiver through their spines.

So, without the comforting presence of their fellow travelers, each boarded a train. And each felt more alone than he had in a lifetime.

My father remembers the solitude of riding that train to its first stop. But even more, he remembers the extraordinary comfort he felt when he descended there, and looking down the platform, saw each of his friends doing just the same. Elated that fate seemed to have blessed them again, they re-boarded the train's separate cars comforted by the fact that they were not alone.

Hours later, as they approached Cologne, my father noticed two MPs entering his wagon. His heart pounded so loudly that he could almost hear it as he nonchalantly studied the nearest window. How does it open? Is it locked? The scenario spun in his head:

He imagined one of the young MPs standing quietly as the other barked, "Papers!" In his mind Willy would not bother with excuses. He wouldn't even reach into his jacket. Instead, with one motion, the window would be thrown open and he, like a mountain lion, would be out before they had a chance to think.

Once confident that the window was not locked, he turned back toward the MPs and studied their actions carefully. He soon realized they were only going up to other German military personnel, just as the other MPs had done in the restaurant earlier that evening.

His pulse returning to normal, my father took a seat. Though he had come to detest the German language that accompanied the torture that had surrounded him in the previous months, he now felt gratitude for the German he'd been taught as a child as he listened to the various conversations that were going on around him. He found himself most aware of the couple in their sixties seated beside him. Before long, the gentleman pulled out an old gold pocket-watch and flipped it open.

"Odd," he said curiously to his wife, "no Gestapo. They always check papers by this time."

135

Realizing the man made the trip often, and that it was only a matter of time until the Gestapo would appear, Willy's heart began pounding anew. But, as capture was no longer an issue, he methodically began to review his plan of escape and felt strangely secure in it, secure in the thought that he would never allow himself to be taken again.

Months later, it was brought to my father's attention that the Gestapo did search the Berlin/Cologne train regularly, in fact every day. But not that fourth miraculous day of Hanukkah when he, Leopold, and Joseph made it safely to Cologne. Apparently, on that day, the only others that boarded, besides passengers, were angels.

Chapter Fourteen

Cousin David — Mirele

Brussels, Winter, 1942

Sometimes days went by without news of friends or family. And no matter the personal struggles and ever-present danger and doom, those were the good days. When my mother's cousin, David Mazur, returned home in Antwerp one day after being out for only a few hours, he discovered to his total emotional destruction that his wife and children had been taken.

Debbie Schiff was acknowledged as a fine catch when David had married her. After all, her father owned a well-known deli in the quarter, one with large vats of pickles that would serve as special treats to children who visited. Their marriage had been a good one, filled with love and commitment.

Learning of the deportation of his wife and children, David was frozen and alone. Just as the nightmarish Judenrat officially tracked the remaining Jews, there was an unofficial information network that passed among those who were hidden, and thus, people could often track down those they needed.

The closest relatives David was able to locate were Mirele and her parents (his aunt and uncle). When he showed up on the doorstep of *Bomma* Abrams's narrow two-story Brussels house, there was no question that he would be taken in.

The already cramped quarters were his sanctuary. *Bomma* Abrams relegated him to the bedroom occupied by my mother and grandparents. They had all been sharing one tiny bed, and now they were four. My grandmother, protecting her daughter's chastity, ordered her to sleep closest to the wall. Beside her lay my grandmother, then grandfather, and young David on the end. My mother remembers those nights with her nose pushed against the wall... yet the memory always seems to bring a smile to her lips, maybe just for the memory's ability to conjure all the love and odd sanity that found its way into the darkness. The commitment of extended family... the love of a mother... the warmth and generosity of *Bomma* Abrams... and all amidst a world gone mad.

David stayed for a while, but though still emotionally lost, eventually moved on.

Chapter Fifteen

Returning Home — Willy

Cologne, the Fifth Day of Hanukkah, 1942

The train pulled into the Cologne station, and many of the passengers began to disembark. Willy and his friends noticed one another on the platform and, with unspoken agreement, decided it best to leave the station through different exits and rejoin one another on the streets. Outside, they quickly reunited and walked to their long-anticipated destination. Having lived in the city prior to immigrating to Antwerp, Joseph knew it well and effortlessly led his two anxious friends toward his wife's address, certain she would help accommodate all their immediate needs.

As they moved through the streets it was Joseph's turn to wonder. How would she react to seeing him? He hadn't set eyes on her since the Nazis had demanded her return to the fatherland. And here he was, returned from the dead.

"I'm not sure if she will be in," Joseph thought out loud, "but we can wait at the house until she returns from work. It is here," he continued, his anxiety mounting, "just around this corner."

And as the men rounded the corner, they didn't see the two-story building he'd described; instead they saw only the shock on Joseph's face as he gestured to the bombed-out ruins of the structure. Only rubble.

"Where would she have gone?" Willy questioned, trying to snap him back into consciousness.

Joseph shook his head numbly.

"You must ask a neighbor," Leopold offered.

"Who?" he responded. "Who should we trust? Who can we trust? These good German citizens?"

They walked slowly down the street until Joseph gained enough confidence to approach a woman sweeping her stoop. He asked if she knew where his wife had moved after the bombing, and was given an area across town. Getting there would not be a problem. They still had some German marks, and Joseph knew the city well. The three boarded a streetcar and waited as the conductor approached them for their tickets. The shock on the conductor's face said it all as she shrieked Joseph's name. And within seconds she also recognized my father as the photographer who had taken her portrait back in Antwerp. The woman was Margaretha Diedrighs, Joseph's wife.

A chance meeting. Just as it had been chance that there had been no Gestapo on the train to Cologne. And chance they had made it out of the camp and safely to Breslau in the first place... and now, chance that the only person who could help them, was standing in front of them on a streetcar moving through city streets teeming with Germans.

"Give me an hour to get off work," Margaretha whispered. "Get off here, I'll meet you then."

The three men exited the car. They all found a strange comfort in the luck that seemed to have replaced the previous misfortune that had landed them in the hell of the camps. Afraid they might arouse suspicion standing in one place for an hour, they began to walk slowly down the streets without a destination. Suddenly they noticed someone speaking with the *Schupo* (city police, who wore large pointed helmets). He seemed to be pointing them out, causing the two *Schupo* to turn toward them with curiosity.

And though the three fugitives had no idea what was said, they certainly knew they weren't going to stand around to find out. Without discussion, my father and his friends took off like lightning. If the police hadn't been suspicious before, the men's guilt-like bolting assured they would be now.

"You! Wait! Stop!" the police yelled as they gave chase.

Willy, Leopold and Joseph responded to the commands by running faster, faster than would seem humanly possible, but by now super-human feats had become their norm. They rounded one corner after another, and the police orders to halt followed closely. Turning yet another corner they found themselves faced with a row of apartments, stores and restaurants. They flew into the first crowded beer tavern they saw. Breathless, but acting nonchalantly just the same, they moved to the back and found an empty table. There they sat, eyes riveted to the door. They waited like that breathlessly, but never saw the policemen again.

For Willy, the surprising absence of fear remained strong during these days. Instead, he felt cautious, with an extraordinarily acute awareness of his surroundings. Thought seemed to be replaced with pure survival instincts. Looking back, he would liken himself to a tiger that could sense any danger in his surroundings, always ready to pounce. With a constant stream of adrenalin pulsing through his veins, the tiger was fierce, and Willy was certain if someone, anyone, would try to take him again, he would most certainly kill them with his bare hands — an odd realization for this erstwhile gentle artist.

As they sat in the tavern, they listened to the men talking politics at other tables. They learned that in the very short time since their escape, the Allies had begun constant bombing attacks on Germany. The English attacked by night, while their American counterparts attacked by day. Apparently, most of Germany had been hit, even Berlin.

When an hour had passed, the men felt safe to leave the tavern and return to their appointed meeting place. As promised,

Margaretha was there waiting for them. She was an anxious combination of nerves, excitement, fear, and questions. As they walked to her new apartment she was shocked to hear the details of their ordeal.

Much had changed for her since returning to the fatherland. She'd accepted that the Nazis would maintain control of her life and that she would never reunite with her Jewish husband. Margaretha told Joseph, along with his fellow travelers, about a new lover — a man working in the resistance whom she was sure would be able to help them.

"You understand I believed I'd never see you again," she quietly added to Joseph sympathetically. "That they'd never allow it?"

Joseph just nodded, and an uncomfortable quiet fell over the four as they continued walking. As an outsider to their opera, Willy felt their marriage seemed a mangled memory with love still sentimentally at its core.

Margaretha finally broke the ice that now separated her from her husband. "There is my apartment." She pointed out a two-story apartment building at the end of the street.

"The owner is a silly old woman. She lives on the ground floor with me. She has the front, and I have the back," Margaretha explained as they approached the building. "We will have a couple of big problems with her. The first is that she's quite taken with the Führer, she even signs '*Heil*, Hitler' to my monthly bill along with her own name. The woman is as much a Nazi as the imbeciles in uniform," and then added, laughing uncomfortably, "maybe more... so if she becomes the very least bit suspicious, we are all," the chuckle ended here and Margaretha stopped for emphasis, "dead."

"We'll be mice... she'll never know we are there," Joseph promised.

"It won't be as easy as you think. The second problem is that she and I share a bathroom that opens off the corridor between our separate living quarters."

"We'll make a plan," said Willy. "We'll make it work."

With that, their newest savior kept her three guests hidden in the crowded back rooms of the apartment. And, as she had worried, use of the bathroom became the most complicated part of their hiding, but as Willy had promised, they "made a plan."

After checking that the coast was clear, Margaretha would stand guard in front of the bathroom door while the men made their visits. It was decided that if the landlady would set foot in the hallway, Joseph's wife would immediately join whoever was in the bathroom, no matter the level of his progress. This would create the ruse that she had been en route to the toilet when seen by the old woman. Moreover, it would thwart the landlady's own plan to visit. The difficulty of the ritual was exacerbated by the fact that the three guests were recovering from starvation and probably also from intestinal infections which made trips to the bathroom abnormally frequent. Their stomachs continued to be bottomless pits, and as they constantly tried to fill them, their bodies seemed to quickly absorb the nutrients needed, and dispose of the rest immediately thereafter. So the days in the back of the Cologne apartment were spent eating non-stop and running regularly to the toilet — each visit a possible threat to all their lives.

His wife's enduring passion, or love, or even perhaps pity from the past enabled Joseph to reclaim his matrimonial bed for the time in Cologne. That tenderness was strangely in contrast to the announcement she casually made upon leaving the apartment the first time after their arrival.

"Joseph, if my boyfriend comes while I'm at work, do not be afraid. He is German, but a deserter from the army, and knows everything about you. He is a good man. Tell him who you are. I know he will help."

The hours she was gone were virtually unbearable. Using the bathroom was restricted to the all-too-infrequent absences of the landlady. Movement within the back rooms was extremely limited and noise prohibited; even a sneeze or light cough would most certainly have brought the Gestapo.

As promised, the young German deserter appeared and Joseph introduced himself first, then Willy and Leopold. The men gave the young man some cash and requested that he buy them whatever "black market" food he could find.

And so the routine began. Each night, Joseph would sleep with his young wife. Each day, Margaretha would leave for work, and her boyfriend would arrive. He would pick up some cash, leave for a while, and return with food — potatoes, bread, salami, or whatever else he might find on the streets that day. The selection was greatly restricted by their lack of food cards. As the days passed, the starved fugitives did nothing but eat, becoming stronger by the hour.

So passed the fifth, sixth, seventh, and eighth days of Hanukkah with miracle after miracle keeping them alive. As their weight and strength increased, so did their desire to resume their journey home. Well aware of the danger posed by the old landlady, they knew they had to cross into Belgium as soon as possible. Once there, they felt certain their options for survival would definitely improve. To this end they requested that, in addition to bringing them food, the young German should search the "black market" and underground for a smuggler to help them cross the border. But each day he returned with less and less confidence.

When a full week had passed, and the three fugitives had begun to look human again, Joseph's wife began to panic; they had all been too lucky for too long. The odds were beginning to frighten her, and she sadly but firmly made her point.

"In German we say, '*Hilf dir selbst dann hilft dir gott*' — God helps those that help themselves." If you stay another day, I fear the Nazis will kill us all. If there is no smuggler to help you over the border, God will find you himself and escort you safely across. I know it in my soul."

"I think she's right," Willy said, aware that, though there was comfort in her quarters, time was inevitably running out. "After all, luck never stays in one place too long."

"We certainly didn't escape to be taken again," Joseph continued.

"Or worse, to be killed," Leopold added.

So, without the consolation of guide or smuggler, Leopold, Joseph, and Willy boarded the streetcar that fate had blessed once before. They took the bus to nearby Aachen, a city closer to the Belgian border.

"From Aachen you must walk to Eupen-Malmédy, a small border town. After you see nothing for a bit, you'll come upon twenty or thirty houses. That's the border." Margaretha's boyfriend's voice followed them as they traveled along the road.

"There you will find two kinds of guards — customs and border police. They will look at your shoes. Try to keep them clean. The customs men will be on foot; the police on bicycles. You can expect to see either kind of guard anywhere along the five-kilometer stretch of road that leads to the border crossing."

By now, the three fugitives were looking more and more like civilian workers, or even plain-clothes Gestapo. They were clean, and no longer quite so gaunt. And they walked with the confidence of men who had challenged death and won. As they took note of the landmarks that had been described to them, they could see the safety of the border a few hundred meters away. All that separated them from Belgium was a pair of military men chatting by the roadside. One was balancing on a bicycle; the other stood holding a second cycle.

"We should keep walking and signal '*Heil*, Hitler,'" Leopold suggested.

"If they move toward us in any way... any way... even to speak, they will surely ask for papers," Joseph began to panic.

"And when they learn we haven't any, they'll surely arrest us," Willy calmly whispered. Arrest not being an option to him, he continued, "So if they say a word," he waited a beat and then stated as a matter of fact, "even one word, you both grab the man standing. Find a way to kill him. I'll take the other. The one on the bicycle."

Willy heard his murderous words as if they belonged to someone else, which, in a sense, they did. They belonged to the tiger that had taken up residence in his psyche the moment the escape began, and that was now directly responsible for his survival. And this wild cat was going to succeed whatever the cost. As Willy approached the military men, in his mind's eye, he saw them

ask for identification and move their hands toward their weapons, and then, quicker than humanly possible, Willy pounced, overtaking the man perched on his cycle. In one swift movement, Willy slid his arm around the man's head — ripping it off his shoulders with Herculean strength.

While his mind played out this vision, in the real world of that country road, Leopold and Joseph raised their right hands in salute. "*Heil*, Hitler," they barked.

There was no response from the two young soldiers. Quite clearly, with no love lost on the great dictator, the two were probably Belgians now forced to work for the German military. The three fugitives continued on as if nothing had happened, though the violent murderous vision my father had played out in his mind would stay with him for decades. What had happened to him? He knew the incidents of the previous months would clearly change any man, but when did the transformation really occur? How did the Nazis manage to rewire his young artist's brain? These questions would haunt him for life.

As they approached the border, hoping to find some aid in crossing it, the men reminded themselves over and over that these small homes annexed by Germany two years before were all once part of Belgium. They eyed each front door carefully, looking for some sign to instill confidence of safety, but there was none. They finally settled on one small home close to the border, relying simply on the hope that these once-Belgian citizens would be open to helping their compatriots. The door opened, and a woman in her mid-forties welcomed them. The men shared their old tale of the ailing mother and their missing furlough papers, and nothing of the truth.

"Shhhh," she responded regardless, showing them the door. "The customs official lives upstairs. You must go immediately!"

House after house, neighbors listened to the men's request before respectfully declining assistance.

"Several others have been killed already," said one apologetically.

"I'm a father. I can't take the risk," said another. "But I'll give you directions."

He gave them a description of the surroundings and the only possible routes across the border. And though the risks of embarking on such a trip alone were enormous, they felt they had no alternative — until the arrival of a fifteen-year-old girl who had somehow heard of their peril.

"I can help you," she promised, "as soon as it becomes a little darker."

147

And as the stars began to shine in the blackened sky, the teen took the three young men into the fields. She stopped not far from a small creek.

"There. When you cross there, through the water, the other side will be Belgium," she said, before disappearing almost faster than she'd appeared.

My father and his companions continued alone into the dark woods toward the creek, assuring themselves that the hardships of their journey were behind them. When they finally arrived at its darkened shore, though the icy night air should have warned them, they were surprised to find it completely frozen. As they began their careful journey over the ice, once too far from one side to turn back, and not near enough to the other, they heard the ominous sounds of cracking ice. And though they took great care, the hairline cracks soon split the ice wide enough to suck all three of them into its freezing waters beneath. Fortunately, the creek was not deep, submerging them only to their shoulders, and after a short struggle, the men were able to work their way onto Belgian soil. Their drenched clothing immediately froze solid in the icy night, making it almost impossible to walk. Each step was a mammoth effort.

Still walking through darkened woods, Willy cleared the way and flinched with pain as a large poisonous thorn entered his hand. He tried to get it out, but in the dark, he realized he would have to wait. Then suddenly, the Belgian highway was in sight. The young men were once again torn with indecision: they all realized they might be safer remaining in the woods' dark cloak, but with that "security" came the fear that they might actually stumble back onto German territory. The choice became simple as they began to walk alongside the road. Ironically, after all the miles they'd traveled, they still found themselves separated from safety by barbed wire. Joseph was chosen to reconnoiter and walked closest to the fence, while his friends stayed hidden in the shadows. Though only a short distance from them, the moonless night hid him completely, so when his friends heard Joseph calling to them, they came running. They were shocked to find that he'd been stopped by someone on the road. Though fear began to pump quickly through their veins, luck was still their companion. After climbing over the fence and facing the stranger, the three began to tell their tale of an ailing mother. The man explained that he too was a Belgian forced to work in Germany, and was presently in the midst of his daily mile-long walk home from his labors. He kindly invited the freezing men to accompany him.

Again, the emotional wounds of the camp seemed to heal ever so slightly as this stranger and his family took them in. They were given dinner by his wife and teenaged daughters; their frozen clothes were placed beside the fire to dry. The girls, one eighteen years old, the other nineteen, prepared beds for them. Now, free from the camps for three weeks, the travelers were no longer skeletons, but once again handsome young men.

By this time, the thorn that had embedded itself into Willy's hand was totally infected. One of the girls offered to operate, and after an extremely long effort, was successful. My father remembers, with a glint in his eye, that he was quite certain there was romantic interest that evening. And the fact that the young men were even having such feelings was a sign that the healing had truly begun, for it has been documented that sexual drive disappeared almost completely in the camps. The young men found themselves very drawn to the girls and whispered among themselves as to whether a sexual proposition would be wise. In the end, it was decided unanimously that sex would have exposed their "Jewishness." They knew well that the Nazis had been all too successful in putting the fear of retribution into

149

anyone with even the slightest desire to help a Jew. There was no way to be certain, but the risk of these kind country people turning them in was both real and strong.

With the young men's fantasies behind them, the sun rose to another day of uncertainty and danger. For Willy in particular, it was urgent to get back to Antwerp. Determined to present Esther's English papers to the authorities, Willy still clung to the hope he might save his wife and daughters from the horrible fate they had, in fact, already experienced. The three men were directed to the nearest tram and told to take it to the Verviers train station. There was no direct route to Antwerp, but in Verviers, they found a train to Brussels that would connect to the smaller Flemish town.

At the crowded station, they purchased their tickets and boarded the train, but it failed to depart as scheduled. They tried to remain nonchalant as they nervously eyed each passenger on the train and, moreover, the large number of uniformed men that milled about their car and the platform directly outside their windows. As one, then another hour went by, they found themselves becoming increasingly tense. Then they learned that a German had been killed, and the train was not to leave before the murderer was apprehended. This meant that the already tight wartime security would be increased. To Willy, Joseph, and Leopold, it clearly drew a dark line between life and death.

Again, minutes began to feel like lifetimes, as they wondered how long it would be before the Gestapo would board demanding, "Papers!"

There was huge relief when the announcement came: "Train to Brussels now departing..." Willy breathed a huge sigh. Within hours he would be in Antwerp.

There, he would find his wife's English documents. He would take them to the German authorities.

150

"We've made a terrible mistake," they would remark.... "She and the children will be released from Auschwitz immediately, today if possible, and brought home."

He would walk out with a huge stone lifted from his heart, counting the days till their return.

These were the thoughts that had fueled his journey when he was malnourished and his fatigue greater than otherwise sufferable. These were the thoughts that had helped him survive the months in the camps. These were the thoughts that had helped him somehow forget how cruel his captors had been. These were the thoughts that he continued to believe, no matter how futile they might have seemed to anyone else.

The three men discussed their next move quietly at the Brussels station. They decided that it was best to board the first train to Antwerp. That city had always been their objective, and they could only wonder how long the angels — who had clearly been with them — would remain their traveling companions with so many others in need.

Disembarking at the Antwerp station, having achieved what had seemed a ridiculous and impossible goal, instilled a new confidence. Willy felt more and more certain that he would never again set foot in a German camp. He knew that he would fly, no matter the risk. And somehow he was certain that that flight would be successful.

Willy thought to himself, "Everyone would do the same if they really knew the truth. They would never peacefully board the transports." And finding a way to let the truth be known became another important aspiration.

Willy, Leopold, and Joseph parted ways as they left the station. Seeing his neighborhood deserted, Willy had another destination in mind — the home of his old friend Georges De Groote. As he knocked on the apartment door, Willy thought

151

fondly of the man's visits after curfew time during the early years of occupation.

The door finally opened and De Groote's mother stood there staring at him as if he were a ghost. For, in fact, she thought he was.

"We were certain you were dead," were the only words she uttered, her face white with surprise. Recovering from her shock, she quickly embraced him with tears in her eyes.

"Come, Willy, come in."

After a similar greeting from her husband and son, Georges, they all sat down at the dining table.

"Tell us. Tell us everything," the older De Groote requested, as his wife brought out a plate of apples, putting them down in the center of the table. She then placed a knife and small plate in front of each of them, as has been civilized custom in Europe for centuries.

They peeled their fruit, and then cut the apples into delicate wedges while listening intently to Willy's extraordinary tale. He, himself, neglected the ritual, and bit directly into the whole apple, devouring it in an instant as had become his fashion since the escape. He spoke even while he chewed, telling them every detail he could remember of the camps and of the horrifying separation from Esther and his daughters he had suffered. When everyone had finished eating their own apples, they sat forward resting on elbows with riveted attention. The story continued to pour from his soul, and the reality of his physical starvation became most obvious to his hosts as he, without thought, picked the peelings from each of their plates and devoured them too, one at a time, never stopping his monologue long enough to chew.

Willy noticed their shock, but was too far beyond adhering to civilized etiquette to bother addressing it. He would later

152

wonder at the confusion they politely didn't mention that night — William, who had been De Groote, Sr.'s boss, with the delicate mannerisms of an artist, reaching greedily across the table and eating their table scraps without a thought.

"Where are my in-laws?" Willy asked, after hearing the Jewish quarter had been *emptied*. "I need to see them."

"They've gone. Benny sent for them and has them hiding with some friends," Madame De Groote offered. "It was a miracle they weren't taken."

Georges continued, "Mirele comes to Antwerp once a month to get her ration cards. It's the only way she can get enough food for her and her parents. She's incredibly courageous. I can't imagine many other girls taking such risks."

"Georges goes with her so they look like a gentile couple," his mother added. "He even wears his police uniform. Much less suspicious that way."

"You're a good friend, Georges. The best," Willy smiled with all the warmth in him. "Can you take me to see them?"

"Tomorrow."

Though the De Grootes were most assuredly terrified of the possible consequences, there was no question that Willy would remain with them for the night. In the morning Georges telephoned Brussels.

"I'll be there at eleven thirty. Don't go anywhere. I've got a surprise!"

At that, my grandmother, who'd always had a sense of things, in addition to an extraordinary attachment to her son-in-law, responded, "Willy is back."

And though travel remained the riskiest of endeavors, Georges escorted my father to Brussels as planned. As the two young men approached the apartment building at 16 Rue des Echelles, they saw Mirele dashing across the street toward the

153

building. She was carrying a bag of the small unrationed fish for her mother to prepare for lunch, but when she saw them, she quickly changed directions and ran into her brother-in-law's arms.

"We've been so afraid. The stories...," she whispered while they embraced. "Come. Mother's been on *schpilkes* (pins and needles) waiting," Mirele continued, while pulling him enthusiastically toward the building.

The homecoming was bittersweet. Here he was, reunited with family at last, but alone. And what right had he to be there, when their daughter and grandchildren were not? Willy could not stop thinking about Esther and the girls, and of any possible plan to save them.

"Georges told me Esther's papers are still at the apartment. Del Croix refused to let him in. I've heard the Swiss consul has taken on representing the English. If I can just get those papers.... I think that maybe she and the girls might have been spared, she being English; perhaps the consul could get word into the camp for me," Willy sounded as if he was trying to convince himself more than the others, who listened intently. But as long as he could see Esther's eyes in front of him, and hear his children's voices, he would hold on to his hope. Hope had kept him breathing. It had been there in the storm that came on the night of the escape, and it had been in the strength within his limbs to run. Without it, he would have died months before.

When Willy called Madame Del Croix later that day from Brussels, angrily telling her what fate had befallen him and his small family, her guilt was so strong that she promised to travel to see him in a couple of days, papers in hand.

While awaiting them, there was much catching up to do. Willy learned that his brother Simon was also in Brussels. A tall, handsome man of about thirty, Simon had lined up with others

154

ordered by the Gestapo for transport to the "work camps."
Then, suddenly out of nowhere, a perfect stranger grabbed him
from the line.

"What are you doing here!?" she screamed like a fishwife.

When he heard her Hungarian accent, he explained in
Hungarian, his own mother tongue, that he was simply doing as
ordered.

"You're not a Jew, you imbecile. You're a Hungarian," she
responded in French, sounding as much of a shrew as possible.
"You're not getting away from me that easily. Now, get out of
this line and come home immediately." And though my uncle
had never set eyes on this woman before, he followed her orders.

Helen Gillot was a moderately unattractive woman with an
eye for this handsome young man. Her own husband was
currently with the TODT workers, and she had much time to
occupy. In taking Simon home that day, little did either of them
realize she would soon become a savior to much of his family.

Willy's first night in Brussels happened to be Christmas night
of 1942, and he was given shelter with his brother in the
apartment of the good-natured Helen. Together, the three
listened to Pope Pius XII's annual message to the world. My
father sat riveted to the speaker as he listened intently, waiting
to hear the Pope reprimand the Germans for the civilian mass
murders, including what would eventually total one and a half
million innocent children. Willy listened intently for some
reference to the atrocities. Some plea on the Pope's part that, in
the very least, good Catholics should immediately withdraw from
serving the monstrous Nazi killing machine. But the only plea
on the Pope's agenda for that evening was instead to the Allies
to stop bombing German churches. Even after all my father
had witnessed in the camps of man's most merciless treatment of
his fellow man, nothing... nothing would be as perplexing as this

icon of holiness remaining silent witness to the murder of children.

On December 26, the very next morning, Willy felt compelled to see one of the leading rabbis still in Brussels. Mirele found his address and took Willy to meet Rabbi Ulman. She sat quietly as Willy told the story of the camps, about the train headed straight to the gas chambers, about the strenuous work, the starvation, the beatings, and the painful deaths. He described the Rauff death vans filled with carbon monoxide, and the fact that men would choose them over another day of life in Hell.

Rabbi Ulman listened for hours and then finally laughed in Willy's face. He went to a nearby cabinet and pulled out various postcards with German postmarks.

"You know, it's not as bad as you say," he said, handing the cards to Willy. "My brother sends me these from the camps. He tells me it's not bad at all."

"Those cards are nothing but propaganda," Willy looked at him with total disbelief. "They know you are an influential man. That the Jews will listen to you. What better spokesperson could they have to assure passive captives? Can't you see?"

Willy's voice got louder and louder as he pleaded with the rabbi. He found himself rising to his feet, anger filling his every pore. He knew he couldn't stay quiet, but what good were his words if they were to be ignored? He felt the urge to punch the old man, but instead fled the apartment. Mirele ran out after him, trying her best to calm him.

Obsessed with telling his story, Willy immediately searched out Professor Chaim Perelman, the head of the Comité de Défense des Juifs en Belgique. He agreed to meet with Willy at his home later that evening. In addition to his secret post, Professor Perelman was an educator at the Free University of Brussels, and would later become world-renowned for his work in rhetoric. He lived right outside the city with his wife, a famous concert pianist who had played with Queen Elizabeth of Belgium, so suspicion never arose when loud music poured from their home, veiling numerous clandestine underground evenings.

Willy and his brother, Simon, arrived at the Perelman home at eight o'clock as instructed. He was delighted to see several people from the underground as well as a few members of the organization's clandestine press. As the music poured from the piano, Willy told his tale. And as he saw the horrified but believing eyes of his audience, he felt that a small part of his silent promise to those left behind in the camps was beginning to be fulfilled. He had been talking for weeks, but now people were finally listening.

Everyone there had friends and family who had been deported, and now, the horrifying reality of their status was sinking in. The room stirred uncomfortably with murmurs of fear, pain, and horror.

"William, you are the first eyewitness we've found," Perelman explained with emotion and resolve. "We suspected it was bad, but never this! We will find a way to help. And soon. I give you my word."

"They believe me," were the only words that ran through Willy's mind over and over again with strange relief. "Someone finally believes me."

Not only did Perelman believe Willy, but the professor held true to his word. Later that same evening, the BBC was sent a coded message by the underground, summarizing Willy's account. Almost immediately thereafter, the BBC made a multi-language evening broadcast that went something like this:

Eyewitness account warns that 99% of those deported will not survive. Women, children and elderly are killed immediately. Work camps are in fact death camps. Captives are worked without sustenance till death. Do not

157

get caught by the Gestapo... and if seized, do *whatever* possible to get away. Escape or face immediate death. No one survives if taken.

Prior to that broadcast, all these simple horrific specifics, now known to be fact, had only been whispered about. And even when whispered about, were quickly dispelled as impossible rumors. After all, who could ever have believed the unfathomable? Furthermore, the Nazis had gone to great effort to maintain their "work camp" myth in order to keep their genocide machine well-oiled. And well-oiled it was. The train transports leaving Western Europe destined for the death camps of Poland and Germany carried nearly one thousand people at a time. By the time of the broadcast, many Jews had already been deported, so the Germans considered the use of the holding camps as essential, efficient, and extremely cost-effective.

Because of the holding camp procedure, by April 19th, 1943, when transport No. 20, originating from the Mechelen camp, began its journey to Auschwitz, enough time had passed that William's warning was well known, and the Jewish Resistance was well prepared to take action. In what the *Encyclopedia of the Holocaust* calls "the single most significant resistance operation carried out by the Jewish underground... the only recorded instance of an armed attack in Europe on a train taking Jews to their death," two hundred and eight men, women, and children were able to flee into the woods that night. And of those two hundred and eight destined for the camps, statistics suggest that only three percent would have survived. Only six people of those two hundred and eight would have lived to experience liberation.

Moreover, from that day onward, individual escapes from the transport trains became increasingly frequent.

Within a couple of days, Madame Del Croix, Willy's guilt-ridden Antwerp landlady, kept her word and traveled to Brussels. An anxious Willy finally had the British papers for Esther and his children in his hands. He and Mirele immediately took the documents to the Swiss Consulate. All his hopes that had fueled his escape came together in this one moment. And there he stood helplessly once again as the consul produced a file that he showed to Willy. In it was correspondence between their office and the Germans regarding Esther's plea for help that Willy had initiated while still at Drancy, a five-month lifetime ago.

"You see, we responded to your correspondence months ago," the Swiss bureaucrat offered with pride.

The Swiss Consulate had written to the Gestapo asking for her, and had received a response stating that the Germans were "unable to locate the woman mentioned." "You see here, they answered us immediately," the Swiss consul continued.

"The Germans have been afraid to hurt the English," Willy begged relentlessly. "Perhaps she is alive. You must do something! Something."

"There is nothing we can do."

"Send a letter to the military headquarters in Antwerp, telling them she's English and has been sent to Auschwitz in error, and that something must be done immediately!" Willy demanded.

"I've explained, Sir, there is nothing we can do," he repeated, stonewalling an impassioned young husband and father who refused to give up hope. "Nothing."

He again, for emphasis, showed Willy the German letter in response. "Her whereabouts are recorded as unknown. How can they return someone whose whereabouts are a mystery? I'm afraid our hands are tied."

Willy's mind flashed back to his first day at Ottmuth, just torn from his young family, searching out the camp elder.

"Have you heard about yesterday's transport to Auschwitz?"
Willy almost pleaded with the camp elder.

"Oh, yes," he'd answered flatly. "The camp was overcrowded.
The train rode straight to the gas chambers."

"My wife... she was English... if she yelled out..."

"When it's overcrowded, no one survives."

Mirele's eyes filled with quiet tears as if she'd heard her
brother-in-law's thoughts about her sister. They both stood
there staring at the Swiss bureaucrat, as if staring long enough
would conjure some change.

"I'm sorry," he said, not so much out of empathy, but as a way
to put closure to their conversation. "There's nothing we can do.
Pardon," and he turned toward the rows of filing cabinets behind
him, replacing the meaningless documents from wherever he'd
taken them.

Willy went totally numb. There was a part of him that had
known, from his conversation the first day in Ottmuth, that he
had lost them all... Esther, and Katie, and Germaineke. That
they'd been murdered their first day in Auschwitz. But there was
that other part, the part that had kept him alive. And that part of
him was overwhelmed with a gnawing pain that would stay with
him for the rest of his life.

Mirele had heard that food packages had reached some of the
camps, and wanted to prepare one for her young husband, who
had now been gone for months. Willy found it unlikely that it
would successfully make it into Izi's hands, but assured her that
if it were possible, he knew how to increase the odds.

"If it looks appealing, the guards will surely take it. Izi will
never see the package," Willy explained. "But if we prepare it to
look inedible... if it looks disgusting enough, as if it had been

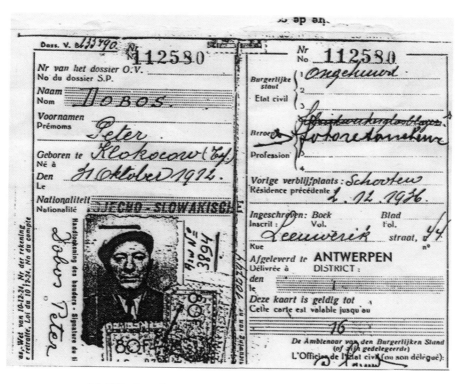

Willy's forged "Peter Dobos"
Identity Card
1942

Belgium   1944

Captain Thiem
Palace Hotel

Mr. & Madame Akard with Captain Thiem
Rixensar

Post-Liberation Brussels, 1944

Willy, Mirele &
Georges De Groote

Willy & Mirele

Benny celebrating
with American soldiers
the day after
Brussels is liberated

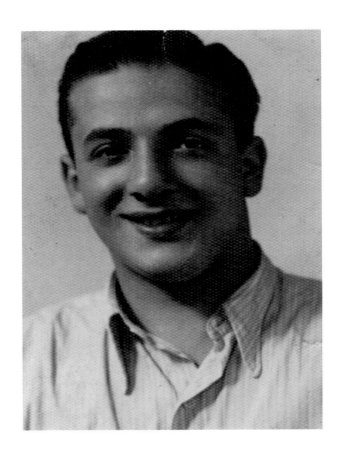

Itzhak Maschkivitzan
born - 1921
deported - 1942
died - in the camps

Esryl (Izi) Anielewicz
born - 1921
married - 1942
deported - 1942
died - Theresienstadt 1945

Madeleine Gotheimer
born - 1923
deported - 1942
died - in the camps

Mirele's parents,
Chaim & Souria

(above)
Before the war

(left)
After the war

Brussels　　1949-55

Willy & Mirele in store

Micheline, me & Suzanne

Front panel of Germaine's
unfinished dress

Postcards from Izi to Mirele

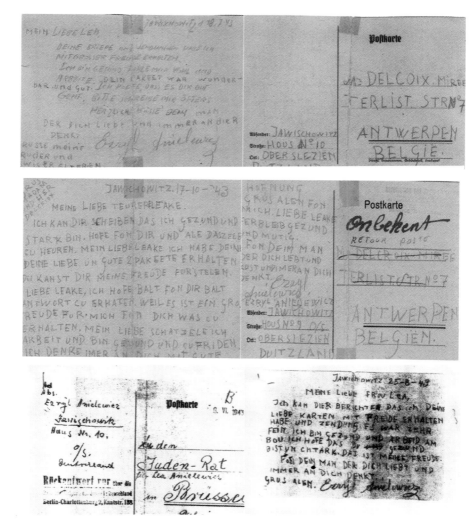

Bottom card is a photocopy, the orginal Orginal is archived in the
U.S.Holocaust Museum, Washington, D.C.

Postcard from Willy to siblings, Otto & Hilda

(written at end of war from Abram's apt. to American foster care facility)

(postmarked May 8th 1945)

Dear Hilda and Otto!

I am very happy that I am able to write a few words.

My wife and children were sent to Poland 2 1/2 years ago. Also Linka, Leo, Miksha, David. From Czechoslovakia the entire family was also deported to Poland. From none of them do we have any news. I fled from Poland.

Write me immediately a response.

Greetings from Simon, Margit & her children.

From your brother, Willy

Mirele and William
in from of "Studio Willy"
Brussels, 1948

DAD and MOM

William
and
Mirele

Université Libre de Bruxelles

Uccle,le 8 janvier 1951
32,rue de la Pêcherie.

FACULTÉ DE PHILOSOPHIE
ET LETTRES
—
50, Avenue F-D. Roosevelt
—

ATTESTATION.

Le soussigné,PERELMAN,Ch.,professeur à l'Université de Bruxelles dirigeant de la section bruxelloise du Comité de Défehse des Juifs, organisme de résistance civile reconnu par la loi,atteste par la présente que

M.HERSKOVIC,William,demeurant actuellement à Bruxelles,146 Bd.Emile Jacqmain,

s'est présenté chez les dirigeants du C.D.J.en décembre 1942, pour leur faire le récit de son évasion d'un camp de Haute Silésie,où il avait été déporté avec sa famille. Il leur a décrit également les conditions d'existence dans ce camp,et fut ainsi le premier témoin oculaire des conditions existant dans les camps d'extermination nazis, dont le témoignage soit parvenu en Belgique. C'est en se basant sur ces renseignements que le soussigné a pu déposer au procès von Falkenhausen.

/Ch.Perelman/

Affidavit from Professor Perelman of the University of Brussels, wherein he states that William was the first eyewitness to return to Belgium from the extermination camps, that he met with the Resistance to describe the atrocities being committed, and that it was based upon his words that Perelman was ultimately able to testify of war crimes committed by German officer Von Falkenhausen

Bel Air Camera, Los Angeles

Willy with brother, Otto, outside
1st Bel Air Camera location
Los Angeles, 1957

Willy and nephew, Samy,
trying out some new equipment
1965

Our Family Today

long-spoiled, the guards' twisted senses might find it amusing to give a starving prisoner spoiled food."

And so they did just that. They prepared a mixture of jams, peanut butter, and coffee grounds. It couldn't have looked much worse. And probably didn't taste much better. Mirele also enclosed socks — but only ones that were well worn, as Willy was certain that socks having any appeal would be seized, too.

When the parcel was ready, Mirele took it to the local *Judenrat*. Here, amidst all the organizational and emotional insanity, she was able to establish his supposed location and the parcel was taken out of her hands. She then asked if there were perhaps any letters from her young husband, and was surprised to hear there were.

"*Liebe Mirele*," began a postcard scripted in German, obviously written by a stranger. Mirele knew at first glance that the handwriting was not Izi's. Moreover, her young husband didn't even speak German. It went on to tell her all was well and that he was working. Two sentences. But the signature she did recognize as his. My mother gained little consolation from this letter written in a foreign language and in a foreign hand, but his signature made her feel some connection. She prepared another parcel as soon as she could, and received yet another, identical note. This routine went on for a while.

Chapter Sixteen

Reunited — Willy and Mirele

"Do what you can, with what you have, where you are."

Theodore Roosevelt

Freedom was a rather odd word for the period that followed Willy's return to Belgium. Though he had escaped the camps, he would never escape the memories of what had been done to him and his family. Moreover, the country was still overrun with Germans, ready to deport him all over again. There was never a real moment of safety, yet for Willy, his determination that he would never allow himself to be taken again, gave him a peculiar liberty. Just like the days of the escape, the clear eyes of his wild tiger were focused on nothing but survival.

An infection, which he'd contracted from the filth in the camps, had developed into a large and painful abscess under one of his arms. He kept waiting for it to heal, but when it didn't seem to, he allowed my mother to take him to a local doctor.

"This will hurt a bit," the doctor warned, beginning to lance it.

But the pain was so intense, Willy lifted his hand to strike him, swearing, "God damn you!"

The words and the violent gesture startled the doctor, but nowhere nearly as much as it startled Willy himself. How was it that he could raise his hand to strike a man bent on helping him? And to swear with words he'd never uttered before? The tiger within him quieted long enough for Willy to regain his composure. As he did, his mind took him back to the camps.

These abscesses were common in Peiskretscham. Men would line up in front of his "friend," the doctor. And though he always remained kind to Willy, toward others he had changed greatly in the short months there. He would scream and shout at the men as he treated them — often seemingly without compassion. Willy later heard that in the time following his escape, the doctor was assigned to care for the Germans' wives and children. Becoming a big *macher*, an important person, he was soon promoted to head Kapo. The previous head — the one who had assaulted Willy for his blanket — highly resented being replaced. He entered the doctor's quarters one day and picked up a chair. Before the doctor could react, it flew down upon his head, killing him instantly.

In the camps, Willy remembered, people were often tortured by being lashed, erratically during the week, but like clockwork on Sundays. The prisoners knew that every Sunday someone would be chosen as not having worked hard enough, or some such "crime." The man would be forced to lie down on a bench. Another man would be made to straddle his legs, and a third, his head, while the victim was whipped with full force. If the Germans were bored that day, they might find it more amusing to have one of the Kapos do the work. A Jew torturing a Jew, now that was entertainment! And if the treatment led to death, well, all the better. The Kapos were often the cruelest of all, and seemed to hit harder than the guards. Willy would learn, after the war, that the Kapo who had beaten him for the blanket offense and later murdered the doctor, was moved to another camp. At Blechhammer in Upper Silesia, the violent Kapo was demoted to mere prisoner status, losing his power and his all-powerful beating stick. To his incredible, albeit earned, misfortune, it was there he came face to face with the brother of a man he had beaten to death at Peiskretscham. This brother tried his own hand at revenge by inflicting frequent, but intentionally never fatal, beatings on the man, now stripped of his weapon and power. By the time the population of the camp was sent on the death march, the Kapo who had killed the doctor and beaten so many, including my father, was now too weak to join and stayed behind awaiting death.

"Willy," Mirele's voice broke into his thoughts. "Willy, are you alright?" Willy suddenly focused on the room around him. He was back in Brussels. Mirele was beside him, and the doctor stood warily in front of him, scalpel still in hand. He looked at them blankly.

"Forgive me," Willy said out loud as he lowered his hand uncomfortably, thinking, "What have they done to me? One day a man, now an animal. What did they do to us all?"

"I understand," the doctor said with trepidation as he approached his patient once again. "Would you like me to help you? You now certainly know it will hurt."

"Yes," Willy responded quietly. Then, "Yes, thank you."

Mirele stood by quietly. She couldn't help but wonder what Willy had seen in the camps. What horror stories hadn't he still told them? She wanted to cry for him, but somehow didn't. It just wasn't her way. Her mind then traveled to her husband. "Was Izi living through what Willy had? Was he suffering that very minute...?" She stopped herself from thinking about it.

After they left the doctor, she never mentioned what had happened there.

"You'll need papers," she offered instead, as they walked down the street. "I've been thinking... I know a man, a clerk in City Hall. Perhaps with a gentile name and your photo, this man can get you an identification card. I've already asked Jacqueline, a friend here in Brussels who owns a pub, for a name you can use. She knows many, many people. Men, actually... many, many

165

men," Mirele smiled conspiratorially. "I style her hair every week. Anyway, she's given me the name of a man and his address in Antwerp. A lover who's apparently returned to Czechoslovakia. Peter Dobos, his name is."

"Peter Dobos," Willy tried on the new name with a strong Czech accent, and after a long moment, "Thank you," he smiled at his young sister-in-law, musing at how much she'd grown up in these short months.

Now in possession of an identity, all that remained was getting to the clerk. Before the war, children of immigrants were required to appear at age fifteen to secure an identity card categorizing them as a "person without a country." If they had been born in Belgium, they were then given the option of taking citizenship at age seventeen. Mirele herself had appeared at City Hall just after her seventeenth birthday to do so.

"Who is this man? It seems he's taken almost every photo put before me," the city clerk had asked when he noticed the Studio Willy signature on the back of her small required photograph.

"My brother-in-law. He's really the best photographer in Antwerp, you know," she relayed proudly.

The conversation had gone on for some time, and as usual, by the end of it she had managed to make a lasting friendly impression on him. Now, nearly a year later, Mirele decided to approach that same man for help during her regular visit to Antwerp to collect her ration cards. She approached him boldly, as one would a dear old friend, and was relieved that he remembered her immediately. She began telling him of her needs, while handing him a newly procured photo of Willy, and Peter's name and address on a small piece of paper.

"I desperately need a false ID card. It's for Willy... my brother-in-law, the photographer... remember him?" she said quietly.

"Shhh," he looked around nervously. "It's gotten far too

dangerous. No false papers. They'd kill me immediately." Then he moved in closer, "Have him go to the police station in Brussels, say he is this Dobos, and that he's just arrived from Antwerp to find his wallet's been stolen with his identification. Say it happened on the train. Have him get a police statement of the theft. Return with that and this photograph, and I'll get you your ID... and it won't be a false one."

He walked away abruptly.

Mirele returned to Brussels and explained the plan to Willy, who quickly followed it.

"My name is Peter Dobos and I would like to report a robbery," he stated angrily at the police desk. "My wallet was stolen from my pocket on the train from Antwerp."

"Did you see the man?"

"No, it was very crowded... I need a new identification as soon as possible."

The policeman started to fill out a form as Willy gave him Dobos's Antwerp address upon demand, but stopped abruptly when he heard "Antwerp."

"Antwerp. I'm sorry, but I cannot issue a new ID here in Brussels," the man explained. "That will have to be done at your local station."

"It's far too dangerous a time to travel back without identification," Willy continued. "Could you give me a copy of what you've written up there — something at least to show the SS if they stop me?"

The policeman scrutinized Willy for a moment.

"They're a bit crazy, you know... not at all logical like you Belgians," Willy offered.

The policeman nodded, agreeing with Willy's observation of their unwelcome oppressors.

"You're right. I guess it wouldn't hurt to give you something," he replied, while handing Willy a copy of the papers he'd prepared. "It is nothing more than your statement anyway, isn't it?"

"Thank you."

Mirele took the police documents back to her acquaintance at City Hall in Antwerp, and an official Peter Dobos identification with Willy's photograph was finally issued.

With identification in hand, Willy momentarily enjoyed a new confidence, which, unfortunately, quickly deflated as he returned to Helen's apartment that evening. Stopping at the corner, he watched a long, black Citroën sedan, a well-recognized trademark of the Gestapo, pull up right across the street. There in the dark, the doors swung open, and the long black coats and tall shining boots of the devil's messengers exited the car and walked straight to a neighboring apartment. Guns at their sides, they pounded on the door aggressively.

"Open," they ordered. "Gestapo."

Willy watched from the shadows as an entire Jewish family was loaded into the car. His eyes darted down the streets and around the corners. He imagined himself the captive, and quickly envisioned his escape. He walked the streets, acknowledging to himself that his escape from Peiskretscham had been a miracle, one that would most likely never occur twice. He reminded himself that if taken by the Gestapo again, the only real chance of survival he had was in running. He walked for hours like that, planning and memorizing the safest escape routes, each street and each turn that would best enable him to elude his pursuers. And when he felt confident in his plan, he went back to the safety of Helen's flat.

Simon and Helen were involved in some sort of dispute, which Simon seemed to laugh off.

"Where have you been?" Simon asked his younger brother.

"With the in-laws. Mirele finally got the ID. Call me Peter from now on," Willy said, tossing the ID onto the table for them to look at.

"Did you see what happened across the street?" Simon asked.

"We heard that someone down the block turned them in," Helen added. "The world's gone absolutely mad. Can you imagine turning in your neighbor to those bastards!?"

"Nothing surprises me anymore," Willy mumbled, thinking there was little evil he couldn't imagine these days. He then turned to Simon with a serious tone, "You know we have to plan a way out, an escape, in case they show up."

He began to look around the apartment the same way as he had the streets.

"You know, if someone turns us in.... Here," he said, pointing to an opening in the ceiling. "We can climb to the rooftops and run. I've got a route planned once we're back on the streets. Come. I'll show you."

Simon looked sheepishly at Helen.

"Go ahead," she said. "I'll get dinner. But come back soon or I'll have you running sooner than you think."

Simon and Willy walked the streets as Willy explained which were the best routes and why. When he was satisfied with their plan, he turned to his big brother.

"So what was Helen yelling about when I walked in?" Willy finally asked.

"She keeps threatening to turn us all in, even your in-laws, too, whenever I don't want to screw her," Simon said, shaking his head. "That's all she wants to do. There's a war on, and all the woman can think of is *shtupping*. She's something else," he finally laughed lovingly.

Willy laughed too. And the sound of his laughter felt strangely foreign, as if it didn't belong to him at all.

"It could be worse."

"How?" Simon asked dejectedly.

"If she wanted me to *shtup* her. She's a good woman, brother. A Godsend...but she's definitely not a beauty."

Willy slapped Simon lovingly on the back.

"Well, if Helen's the best He can send, He's got a hell of a sense of humor."

"Most of what He does these days has become a mystery," Willy responded, no longer laughing.

Maybe because this was the first time he really laughed out loud since being deported, it was the first time he became acutely aware of his need to cut it off — of the fact that he would no longer allow himself that indulgence. How could he? What right had he? He was there, breathing, while those he loved were gone. Breathing, he felt, was moderately acceptable... but laughing? Not at all.

Simon saw something strange come over his brother, but had no idea what it was.

"Come on," he said smiling. "Let's go back. We don't want Helen angry at us both."

A few days later Willy was en route to see his in-laws at the Abrams's apartment. Still a block away, he noticed a sight more dreaded than the black Citroën — military trucks, several of them lining the streets in front of the apartment. His eyes moved across the street, where he saw a dozen soldiers on the rooftops. Their rifles aimed directly at his in-laws' apartment. After what seemed an eternity, Willy saw the men quickly descend the roofs, get back into their trucks and speed away.

The street was shrouded with a dead silence as it always was after one of these raids, almost as if the entire drama had never actually played out at all.

After waiting until he felt it would be safe, Willy ascended the small staircase to the apartment where he found an aftermath of strained chaos. Mirele was obviously shaken, her father had become incontinent when the guards had stormed, and her mother was yelling incomprehensively at Benny.

"Mama... it's over. Please leave me alone. I can't hear myself think," Benny implored.

The impetus for the less-than-friendly visit was more complicated than most such raids. Benny's professional gambling career had been little hindered by the war. On the contrary, it often provided the funds my mother needed to keep their parents alive. But, during a recent visit to the dog races, he was stopped and asked to present his papers — which were, naturally, false. He was arrested, and it was discovered that he was a Jew, with forged papers. Unfortunately, or perhaps fortunately, the investigating officer now on his case discovered that Benny was carrying diamonds, the dealing in which was his secondary trade, or possibly third, depending on how one would break down his ever-busy schedule. Another was his extraordinary skill as a confidence man — an ability that proved extremely helpful while being interrogated by this man, who was one of the many self-serving Nazis. For, though the Führer was loved by his loyal Nazis, he and the Reich often came second to personal gain in this cadre of extremely *moral* followers.

The investigator became fixated on the man who had issued the false papers. The actual forger was one of Benny's friends — and for Benny, loyalty was law. Fast talker that he was, Benny began a tale of a mysterious forger who frequented the tracks — easily recognizable, but whose name and residence were unknown. In exchange for his own freedom, Benny promised he would help them apprehend the culprit.

After confiscating Benny's diamonds, a bargain was struck.

171

Benny was to show up daily at the track, which, of course, he would do with pleasure. The day he spotted and fingered the forger for them (his lie), he would be completely free (their lie). He was to report to this officer daily.

The first visit thereafter, Benny casually took a diamond stickpin from his lapel and placed it in the lapel of the investigating officer.

"You know, neither of us has any real idea how this war will end up," Benny philosophized. "We both are rather well connected on our respective sides. So I propose a commitment to each other, a contract of sorts. If my side prevails, I will assure you safe harbor. If yours remains victorious, you'll do the same for me. The world has become quite a dangerous place; I'm sure you could use a friend."

Unfortunately, another German officer got wind of Benny's doings and traced him to the home of *Bomma* Abrams, which in turn led to the Gestapo's arrival at the house that fateful evening. The officer immediately "confiscated" the diamonds that Benny was holding. Wanting to be certain no one higher up would ever know, as the officer had little intention of turning them in, Benny's "plain sight" murder seemed to be the officer's most logical solution. To that end he demanded that Benny go to the roof. If it looked like an attempted escape, the young soldiers across the way would shoot on sight. But as no one can con a con, Benny understood quite well what the officer was doing. If he brought Benny in alive, he would have to turn the diamonds over to his superiors for fear of discovery. And since Benny was a gambler, he bet his life on the fact that the diamonds meant more to the officer than one more prisoner... so there they stood at stalemate.

Frustrated, the officer finally demanded everyone's papers. My mother climbed to where she had them hidden in a ceiling panel. She pulled them out cautiously and turned them over. The officer studied each one carefully. There was one for my grandmother, one for my grandfather, one for my mother, and four others bearing the names of Willy, Esther, and the girls — the ones that had been brought to him from Antwerp by the elderly Mme. Del Croix.

"Who is William Herskovic?" the officer barked. "Where is he?"

"He's my brother-in-law," Mirele offered nervously. "He was taken to the camps six months ago."

"You are using this for rations!" he screamed. "Your brother-in-law is in the camps and you are eating his food, you *schwein*, you disgust me."

Then, staring straight at Benny, he continued, "You, *Jude*, you and your sister will report every day to the Gestapo until that forger of yours turns up." When emphasizing, "and your sister," he turned and glared at the terrified teen. "You understand," he barked, as if it was not a question.

He abruptly turned and left the apartment, his pockets loaded with Benny's jewels, returned to the street, called off his gunman, and all three trucks pulled away in unison.

Peace or war, money remained a necessity of survival. My father knew he would have to live in the shadows for the time being, so he searched the city for the best photographer and approached the man to ask for retouching work.

"I'm sorry, I already have enough men working for me," the man brushed him off.

Willy picked up a pile of photographs on the counter.

"Let me take these. I'll do the work and if you're not happy, you won't pay. If you like what you see, we'll discuss things again."

173

The man nodded slightly, "As you like, then. But no promises."

When Willy returned with his work, certain of its superiority, he wasn't surprised to be hired on the spot. The man gladly paid him for what he'd done and handed over the next order. Willy continued this arrangement, traveling back and forth to the shop by bus until the day it was halted without warning. The Gestapo came aboard with their usual gruffness, and Willy felt as if a noose was tightening around his neck as he was ordered off the city transport with the other passengers. They were all forced to stand against a nearby wall, faces just inches from it. All the torture of the camps flashed in front of his eyes. The humiliations that he constantly tried to bury. The fear that he'd pushed down away from his psyche. But there it was again, clearly at the forefront of his thoughts as the men in black boots and long coats harassed the passengers.

"Papers," they demanded.

"What are you doing on this bus?"

"What is your business?"

"Who were you visiting?"

Questions were fired at each nervous man or woman, one at a time with their noses to the wall. Then, just as suddenly as the Gestapo had appeared, they left. Some passengers walked away angrily, put off by the continual Nazi oppression; some simply boarded the bus again.

Though Willy was one of those who got on again, as the bus pulled back onto the streets, his mind reeled. He could not, and would not, risk this again. So, because Mirele was young, self-assured and now a bleached blond easily passing as a gentile, Willy asked for her help.

"There is a photo shop nearby; do you think you could go in and tell the owner that you've an invalid brother who's an artist in need of work," Willy asked his sister-in-law. "No one seems to be suspicious of you... besides, you're a young woman, and I'm sure he'll be more prone to give work to you, than to me."

Mirele was happy to make the effort, and sure enough, the old photographer decided to give it a chance. And, when he saw the incredible quality of the work Mirele returned to him the next day, a daily routine began. Mirele would pick up new photos, and drop off those Willy had completed. Though the proprietor was always delighted with the work, he never really accepted her tale.

He would often look the young girl in the eye and state simply, "I think there's something hidden in your story. A little star, perhaps...."

She would tell him she hadn't any idea what he was talking about. He would study the perfect retouching, shrug his shoulders and hand her a new workload. And so it continued.

Though Willy slept at Helen's, he would work all day in Abrams's tiny apartment. Even before the war, my grandparents had become like parents to him, and welcomed him lovingly. And though there was some comfort in the routine, Willy's anxiety continued to build. The Gestapo seemed to be visiting Helen's neighborhood more frequently, usually on the tip-off of a local sympathizer. Whether motivated by hate or fear, the result was the same. And after witnessing the Gestapo's rather dramatic visit to the apartment that housed his in-laws, things felt even more precarious. To this was added the anxiety surrounding the regular required visits to the Gestapo by Benny and Mirele.

Willy felt that he had to find some alternatives, so he decided to track down his stepmother's sister, Margaret, whom he had heard was in hiding nearby. Her husband had already been deported and would eventually die in the camps, and her three young daughters were secreted with three different families. Willy visited Margaret and asked if she had any idea as to where he might be safer. She sent him to the family caring for one of her girls, but they had just heard a rumor that the Gestapo might call upon them, so they declined. The police did in fact arrive aggressively at their door the next day, but fortunately for all concerned, believed the story that the child was their own, and left in short order. Willy's presence there surely would have been the end to them all.

On his way back to my mother's, he noticed a sign:
HIRING WORKERS TO GO TO FRANCE
Willy entered the storefront and learned that civilian workers were being sent to do paid manual labor in France for the German Army. He quickly decided there would be no better place to hide from the Nazis than under their very noses.

"When would we be leaving?"

"Today."

Willy quickly went to prepare his departure, content with the opportunities the work offered. He felt strangely safe, believing the Germans wouldn't think to question one of their workers about being Jewish — what Jew would be courageous enough to hide under their noses? But, more than that, Willy became excited about the possibility of securing additional information for Perelman and the underground.

He looked for the oldest valise he could find; something that a local peasant would carry. He then visited a pawnshop and purchased an extremely worn saw — a complicated contraption that only a third-generation craftsman might have inherited. He purposely tied the old tool to the outside of the suitcase and returned to the office just in time to board the train.

Traveling as the Czech gentile, Peter Dobos, he had passed over the Belgian border into France and very soon arrived at his destination — a rolling hillside somewhere between Lille and the northern coast.

Willy made a point of speaking only Czech and French. Not many of the workers spoke German, so Willy knew there was a possibility that the Germans would speak freely around him if they didn't know he spoke their language.

Noticing that most of the officers seemed to stay around the camouflaged area, he volunteered to work with the group that was given the job of rigging camouflage around small hillsides. Eavesdropping at every opportunity, he heard the officers discussing missiles. The workers knew they were camouflaging, but had no idea of the gravity of their task. My father soon learned that he was partaking in the construction of a secret missile launcher. The Germans were preparing to use something Willy would later understand to be the newly developed V–1 rockets. The plan was to launch missiles across the channel to London. Willy's specific work was to cover the exterior part of the launchers' tracks. The balance of the tracks was carved into the hillside. The mechanism was set up so that a missile would be shot out, and the launcher quickly retracted into the hillside, where it would remain undetected.

Once he realized the importance of this information, Willy did his daily work, impatiently awaiting his first furlough, anxious to bring the news to the underground. During his first trip back to Brussels, my father drew every detail of the set-up that he could remember, and immediately took his designs to a delighted Perelman. Hoping to learn more, Willy returned to his job as scheduled.

Shortly afterwards, also nervous about the safety of living in Brussels, his brother Simon showed up at the worksite as well. Willy made sure that no one knew they were brothers, especially since the names on their identification cards did not reflect it.

Chapter Seventeen

To the Countryside — Mirele

Spring, 1944

Mirele's required visits to the Gestapo were beginning to wear on her more and more. She wondered how long they would allow the young Jewish girl to return to her apartment, when most others were being deported. How long would the officer believe Benny's promise? Or how long would they even care about it? Mirele finally decided she and her family all had to disappear, and fast.

Her first task was to convince Benny to join Willy and Simon in the workforce. Her second was getting him safely there. She'd seen Willy's expert work in forging identification cards, which he had done for many during his time hiding in Brussels, and she tried to imitate it — "tried" being the operative word. Though she did her best in duplicating the stamp by hand as her brother-in-law had done, the results were rather comical.

"Are you trying to get me killed?" Benny asked laughingly when he saw the botched effort. He tore off the photo, still chuckling, "Thank you, sister dear, but I'm sure *nothing* will be better than this."

Benny, too, had tired of the daily visits to the Gestapo, so with or without believable papers, he decided to follow his baby sister's orders and joined Simon and Willy at the worksite in the French hills.

With Benny gone, Mirele knew she certainly couldn't return to the Gestapo alone, and decided it was best for her and her parents to leave the city immediately. Being so young and a new resident in Brussels, she had very few friendships to call on. She remembered the kind doctor who had treated Willy's abscess the year before, and went to appeal to him.

"I'll happily take you in," the doctor offered kindly. "You could easily pass as my daughter. But I'm afraid I can't help your parents. It's far too risky."

She knew the doctor was right. Looking like a gentile teen and speaking both French and Flemish perfectly, Mirele would have had little trouble finding shelter. Her parents, however, were much too conspicuous, due to their age and strong foreign accents. So, with no intention of deserting them, Mirele turned to Helen. Mirele asked this woman, who'd become a friend to them all, if she might know of someone able to hide her and her parents outside the city.

Helen was quick with a plan. She happily took the three to Rixensar, a small village around thirty miles from Brussels, where her own in-laws resided.

"It's already been raided.... All the Jews living there have already been deported. I'm sure the Germans will leave it alone," Helen assured them. "Besides, it's a village of some size. I'm sure we'll find something."

The absurdity of hiding her lover's brother's in-laws with her husband's family was lost on no one. But neither was the kindness. Unfortunately, as they wandered about the village, she was disappointed with the trouble they had in finding anyone to take in the small family, even while keeping their Jewishness a secret. Finally, with almost all their options gone, they came to a small convenience store named Del Hase, which happened to have a second-floor apartment for rent. Helen and Mirele visited with the proprietess, an older woman, Madame Linchamps. Finding she was hesitant to rent to strangers, Helen rambled on and on about her own husband, emphasizing that he was a town local who was forced into servitude, and whatever else she could conjure up until she finally persuaded Linchamps that the newcomers were a safe bet.

Living there as gentiles, Mirele, in a very short space of time, had ingratiated herself with her landlady, helping the older woman in whatever ways she could. She washed floors, did laundry, and even styled the woman's hair. My grandmother often helped with the cooking, and soon they all found themselves living as friends. They would eat together every day, and share gossip about the neighbors.

Chapter Eighteen

Hiding in Plain Sight — Willy

France, Spring, 1944

Back in France, Willy continued to pretend he had only a casual relationship with Simon. One particular day, all the workers were sitting under the trees eating lunch when several men next to Willy began to talk freely about his brother, who was going under the name of André Gillot (Helen's husband's name).

"I don't get it... this Gillot has such a strong accent," one man mused.

"You're right. Gillot is a French name, and he certainly doesn't sound like a Frenchman," another agreed.

Wanting to stop the suspicious conversation immediately, Willy joined in.

"I met him in Brussels before the war. He's married to this crazy Hungarian woman who refuses to feed him if he speaks anything but Hungarian at home. Seems it's ruined his French."

"To make him lose his accent, she's probably refused him a lot more than just supper," the first added.

While Willy laughed along with all the others, he suddenly saw Benny walking toward him. Knowing it might be to their advantage to be "strangers" to each other, Willy made no effort to acknowledge the new arrival. Benny, observing this and the fact that Willy and Simon were sitting apart from one another, quickly caught on. After all, deception was one of his more perfected crafts.

Though Willy had become used to witnessing luck, the days

that followed were in some ways the most miraculous of all, for men like Benny and Simon were truly not made for manual labor. Like Willy before them, they, too, were posted on camouflage. The missile launchers were to be hidden behind large nets, and the nets had to be covered with foliage. Their jobs were to weave leaves through the netting. Simon worked slower than anyone believed possible, and Benny, for his part, decided not to separate his loyalties from his productivity. The idea of advancing the Nazi cause in even the slightest way was abhorrent, so he spent one minute lacing in the greenery, and the subsequent two minutes taking it out again. Had this happened in the labor camps it would have led to his death; here, he was simply reprimanded for his ineptitude.

The three spent as little time together as possible to avoid making any mistakes that would give them away. When an occasion arose that they might be positioned next to one another for the day's labor, Simon would often slip into Yiddish and even use Willy's real name. These slip-ups terrified my father, for he imagined that if their true identity as Jews would have been revealed, they would have been sentenced to something far more painful and horrible than death.

Benny was what some might compassionately call "high-strung," building tension even under normal circumstances. However, here at the Nazi worksite, it soon flared into outright paranoia. Not that paranoia was particularly out of place in their current situation. Unfortunately, Benny's anxiety about the Gestapo officer he'd left behind in Brussels turned into a fixation, and the German's threats haunted him, never leaving his thoughts for a single moment.

"He must be furious by now that I stopped reporting in," he told Willy quietly one evening. "I'm sure he'll find me. He has the ability, you know."

184

"Don't be ridiculous," Willy tried to calm him. "There's no way he'd track you here. It's absurd."

"What do you think? When Mirele goes in without me. How many days will he believe her excuses? He'll force her to tell him. He'll threaten her, or worse. She'll have no choice but to tell him. How could I have left her?"

As much as Willy didn't want to think along these lines, Benny's words began to resonate. He knew first-hand the relentless ways of the Nazis.

"We have to leave this place now," Benny insisted. "Paris is our only chance. I have friends there. We'll be safe. We'll send for my sister immediately."

"Fine. We'll go tomorrow."

Leaving without permission was not easy, but getting it was complicated, so Willy and Benny took their few belongings and snuck out just before dawn. They walked the 35 kilometers to the station at Lille, and waited for the next train departing for Paris. Moments after they boarded, it was Willy's turn to panic. His French was nowhere nearly as good as Benny's, and his ability to remain anonymous there would be just as inferior. Willy decided he felt much safer as a Czech worker under the Nazis' noses than wandering the unfamiliar streets of Paris, so he grabbed his small case and jumped back onto the platform. But Benny's con man talents quickly brought him back onto the train.

Willy stood there at the entrance and nervously reviewed his options.

"All aboard," the whistle warned, and Willy suddenly jumped off again.

"Paris is right for you... not me. Be safe," Willy waved to Benny as the train pulled away. "I know this is best for us both."

Willy then ran all the way back to the work camp. When he

arrived at his bunk, he was shocked to see everything cleared away.

"What happened?" he asked one of the workers as he was leaving.

"Oh, Peter, there you are. The Germans came and picked up all your things," the man offered. "Your case was gone. We told them you'd run off."

Willy's justified fear of being conspicuous was now outweighed by the necessity to carry off a believable false identity. He thought that a gentile worker would be indignant, perhaps even furious. Any suspicions regarding his identity would be diminished if he confronted the authorities angrily.

"I leave for two hours to see a doctor," Willy complained, "and you empty my bunk?!"

"We were told you'd run off."

By fortunate coincidence, Willy had been accidentally pushed off a high pile of rails the day before. Knowing there had been many witnesses, he reminded them of the injury, and pointed out the absurdity of their actions. The bottom line was that he was back and ready to work, and as far as they were concerned they needed labor. Within minutes he was back on the job.

Willy ate his lunch that day while listening to the tales of some new arrivals — Belgians who had left the TODT service.

"Couldn't take the job another day," one man told the others. "The things we saw were unbearable... these Germans can be monsters." Urged to go on, he did, but in an extremely quiet voice, certain that criticism was something the nearby German soldiers would not take too well.

"We would be minding our business working in the forest, when the soldiers would come through. Once they came with many Jewish children. We were commanded by the superior to make a fire. 'Larger,' he yelled, as we worked up the flames.

And when it was big enough to suit him, we heard words none of us will ever forget. 'Toss them in,' he yelled to his soldiers. And they did. Can you believe it? The cries of the children were intolerable." The worker paused as if trying to believe he'd actually seen such insanity, then continued, "The kinder men, they would smash the children's heads hard against the tree trunks before they'd throw them in. That was their kind gesture. The most evil would use the children like clay pigeons for target practice... one would toss a small infant into the air toward the fire pit, another would shoot him mid-air before he'd land into the flames." The Belgian paused even longer this time, and when he continued it was almost to himself, "I couldn't bear it anymore."

Willy quietly sat nearby and tried to hide the tears that burned the inside of his eyelids. He tried to hide the pain that pulsed through him as he remembered his two girls — fourteen months and four years old. Suddenly, he could hear their laughter. Little Katie was clinging to his legs while he worked in the studio. Tiny Germaineke was sleeping peacefully in his arms, her small head resting on his shoulder. A small wet spot lingered on his shirt from where she had suckled the fabric to soothe the pain of teething. And then the screams. The screams that would never leave him for a lifetime.

"Daddy, please don't leave me!" Katie had cried out as he was torn from the cattle car that would drive her to a certain death.

He prayed that her fate had been kinder than that described by the Belgian. He prayed that there had been no suffering. He prayed that his babies never realized what fate had befallen them, and he prayed that as certain as he was that Hell was now on earth, that there was also a heaven where they had found peace.

"Planes," a loud voice wailed an order: "Hide!"

187

Everyone scrambled from where they were, a routine that was becoming more and more frequent. The English and American planes would fly over them, most probably photographing their work, and the men ran to the nearby hills for cover, but my father would remain behind.

"Peter, come on," the others yelled. "Are you crazy? Do you want a bomb to fall on top of you?"

He never explained that was exactly what he hoped for — that the bombs would fall. That maybe him being there would facilitate it. It would be worth dying to see the bombs drop. Nothing would have made him happier than to see the missile launchers destroyed before their completion, and possibly Germany's chance of victory in the process.

Finally, in May of 1944, only weeks before the momentous D-Day that would put Normandy into the world's consciousness forever, my father and Uncle Simon were given their weekend furloughs. They traveled with several other workers by truck to Lille. The sun had already begun to set as they were to continue their journey to Brussels on the seven o'clock train, when air-raid sirens began to wail.

Everyone at the station was herded into a bomb shelter, which had been constructed below. As my father and uncle made their way in, they found the shelter was already filled with people. There appeared to be a preponderance of German officers with just a few civilians in their midst. Tables and chairs filled the space, and people quickly settled into them in close proximity to one another. Willy listened attentively to those around him with the heightened sensibility and interest that had become his way, honing in on a nearby conversation being carried on between two concerned officers.

"Paris yesterday... a train on the way back to Brussels, the filthy Americans bombed it," reported one officer.

"But the train roof is reinforced with steel," said another. "That must have helped?"

"Unfortunately not. The Americans have new automatic weapons that can penetrate the shielding," the first continued, disheartened. "We had many casualties. I'm sure that's behind this siren today. Trying to take fewer risks."

"Do you think it's safe to board?"

"Of course not," he laughed the nervous laugh of a man walking into fire, "but what choice have we?"

The tenor of their voices became strained with disillusionment. Things were not going exactly as planned. The Germans' "certain victory" was suddenly far from certain, and the realities of war were becoming uncomfortable for everyone. In these words of German military disappointment came enormous hope for my father. Hearing the officers speak of their fears of defeat was music to his ears. And the thought of the Americans as victors gave him renewed life.

When Willy and Simon returned to Helen's apartment in Brussels, they learned that Willy's in-laws had moved to Rixensar.

"I believe the owner of the shop where they are living has a nearby house with rooms to rent," Helen offered Willy. "Maybe it would be safer for you there."

Willy thought that being in a rural area seemed a good idea, especially in light of the Germans' words. If the Allies were getting more aggressive, the occupied cities were likely to become more dangerous. He had also grown to enjoy the warmth of being with Mirele and her parents, so he departed on the next bus.

Being alone with his thoughts had become difficult, and as he traveled into the green countryside, his thoughts moved surreally back and forth through time and emotions. It was not even two years since he'd been deported, yet everything had drastically changed, and moreover, nothing would ever again be the same.

From all he was hearing on the streets and on the radio, Willy felt an Allied landing was inevitable. With that, the end of the war might actually be forthcoming, and if so, it would be in explosions of bombs, guns, and human destruction. He could only pray for the Allies' victory, and in that light, it seemed the right time to make sure his loyalties were clear to any he might come across by ending his work for the Germans at the missile launchers. Ironically, he would know how accurate he'd been only weeks later, when devastation fell upon the northern French coast — only miles from that very area where he'd been working. In the meanwhile, he felt confident that if he were to be stopped, his furlough papers would ensure his safety.

Chapter Nineteen

Together in Rixensar — Willy and Mirele

Rixensar, 1944

By the time of Willy's arrival in May of 1944, the bond between Del Hase's proprietors and his in-laws was well-established. Madame and Monsieur Linchamps were delighted with the companionship of my grandparents, and they were especially enamored of young Mirele. Though she had matured enormously during the past four years, she was still a twenty-year-old girl possessing all the energy and laughter that comes with youth. And as the Linchamps couple had not a clue that the family they were harboring was Jewish, the relationship was open and comfortable.

When my father arrived, he was introduced as a Czech friend on work-leave. And though Madame Linchamps was happy to make his acquaintance, she had to apologize for a lack of room.

"But you know," she offered, "my aunt lives just next door. I believe she might be willing to let a room."

Her aunt, Madame Ackard, was as kind as could be.

"I only have space in the attic. But if it works for you, I'd be happy to rent it."

The room was sparse, but better than most of Willy's recent dwellings. He quickly came to admire the relationship Mirele had forged with their hosts and decided to do the same. Anything he could do for Madame Ackard, or even the Linchamps, he did willingly and happily.

He spent most evenings at the Linchamps with Mirele and her parents. And it was on one such evening, just weeks later, that they all sat attentively around the radio, though strictly forbidden, listening to the BBC announcement of the invasion of Normandy. As Belgians, they all felt a strong and unified sense of triumph as they heard a detailed description of the strategic victory of the Allies. Willy quietly wondered if his information and drawings of the missile launchers had ever made their way from the underground to Allied intelligence, and if that knowledge could have played some part in the strategy of the attack.

Just across the way, a room had been rented to a Belgian, who had entered the German forces and become a rather intolerable Nazi. He only recently had moved there with his wife and seventeen-year-old daughter to hide from their old Belgian friends who'd found his allegiance insufferable. After the neighborhood elation over the invasion of Normandy, Willy spent some time with the man. And though telling him nothing about himself, he would listen to the Belgian traitor's fears.

"We've come here, you know, because of this," the man offered nervously one particular day. "This seemed the safest place for us if the Germans are pushed out. I'm afraid I won't be held with affection by my old neighbors."

Willy silently wondered how this man could have gone against his own countrymen.

"It shouldn't be all too bad for you," Willy said cautiously, deciding to comfort instead of condemn. "Once there is victory, all the foes will try to find a connection again. It will ultimately be about commerce for the Americans and Russians... You'll see, there will eventually be some settlement with Germany."

The degree of this man's evil became strangely inconsequential to Willy as he listened to his own words, becoming saddened by the reality they represented. One day this would be all over, he thought — governments will settle into new arrangements, and there he would be, alone, without his wife and daughters.

After the news of Normandy, more and more time was passed listening to the regular BBC broadcasts — still forbidden by the German military, of course, who knew that the more possible the chance of liberation, the more difficult control would become. To assure the people's adherence to this ban, the Nazis would send out special trucks equipped to detect broadcast reception. When they found a group listening to foreign broadcasts, soldiers would enter aggressively and arrest the offenders. But at this point, news of Allied victories meant more than life to Willy, making it impossible to tear himself away. So, even though the radio announcers alternated between languages, my father, who understood nine of them, would listen constantly.

One evening, as Willy, Mirele, and my grandparents sat with their landlords and listened, his head suddenly began to spin.

"Majdanek has been liberated," the radio voice declared and then went on to describe the camp in the words of the soldiers who'd been there.

"Evidence and reports of mass murder. The living are walking corpses... one huge room piled to the ceiling with children's shoes."

Sometimes we can hide in uncertainty, and such was how my father had clung to sanity. But sadly, the buffer that uncertainty may permit is quickly destroyed with fact.

"Piled to the ceiling with children's shoes" echoed in Willy's mind again and again. "Children's shoes," his head ached. His children's shoes. Katie and Germaineke's tiny shoes.

The buffer was gone. The reality and the pain it brought into the Linchamps's living room that night pressed against his heart. Against his psyche. He fell to pieces there in the peasant home of a gentile family somewhere in the Belgian countryside. They watched in amazement as the tears began to pour from his soul.

"Look at Peter crying," said Monsieur Linchamps, referring to Willy by the false name he'd been living under. "Don't be so silly, Peter, the war is almost over... the deaths... these were only Jews," he attempted to console. Willy couldn't even look the man in the eye. He knew the peasant had no comprehension of what was going on, of the inhumanity of his own words, and worse yet, his thoughts. Maybe he was the voice of the thousands that allowed the destruction in the first place. Willy couldn't even hate Linchamps. He was basically a good man; he simply did not believe the death of a Jew was worth a tear. And never, in his wildest imagination, would he have dreamt that one of his guests that evening may have actually lovingly laced, or perhaps fastened a tiny buckle, on a pair of those children's shoes.

As the Allies' triumphs became more frequent, my father's optimism and entrepreneurial drive kicked in. He quickly designed a brooch that would personify the victors. It began with a miniature picture frame — a dove perched on the top, and the word "Liberté" inscribed below. To fit inside the frame, Willy created a photograph compiled of four portraits: De Gaulle, Roosevelt, Churchill, and Stalin, their respective flags flying above each of their faces. He ordered ten thousand copper pins, and while they were being made, he printed the same number of his photograph combination. Once the brooches arrived, he spent weeks placing one photo into each. All this helped pass the long summer days.

When he wasn't working on the liberation pins, my father would often read outside, with the sun falling gently on his back. The neighboring Nazi's seventeen-year-old daughter would come and lie nearby. She would often remove her bra and be there half-naked beside him. She was quite beautiful, but the stakes of any type of reaction on Willy's part were much too huge to ignore. But whether he realized it or not, the attraction somehow illustrated that he was coming alive again.

One day, he noticed that he wasn't alone in his admiration. He had heard a noise that took his eyes to a nearby chicken coop. There, lying on the ground and peeking through the splintered slats of wood, was his seventy-two-year-old father-in-law. Willy couldn't help but laugh as the poor man tried to scurry away.... It was one of the first laughs he'd had since his arrival in the village. The story would in fact keep them all laughing for some time.

The Nazis constantly patrolled the area, and though defeat seemed near, they still most certainly posed a threat to my parents and grandparents. The four of them knew that no matter how close they felt to these kind strangers, their identity as Jews had to remain a secret. My grandparents had a rather passionate relationship that was punctuated with frequent yelling matches. Unfortunately, when anger flared and voices were raised, they'd find their passions best expressed in Yiddish.

"You know, Mariche," a puzzled Madame Linchamps once addressed my mother with the pet name she'd given her, "when your parents fight, sometimes I don't understand a word of what they are saying."

My mother was quick to respond, "Oh, of course. You know they are from a village where the accent is very tough to understand. Especially when they get excited like they do."

As the months went by, none of the locals ever questioned why my father didn't return to his job on the front. It was quite clear to everyone that he had never been a "sympathizer," and therefore had only worked under duress. Since the Allies had invaded as he'd imagined they would, Willy stayed firm on his decision that it was safest to remain as far from the Germans as possible.

The Nazis, fearing that they would soon be retreating, would pour through these small villages looking for any members of the Resistance who might try to prevent them from doing so. Hoping to catch them off-guard, small units of German soldiers would enter homes with rifles drawn.

Everyone had heard of such raids, and one evening my father looked out the window of his small attic room and noticed two such soldiers outside his own front door. He waited for the knock at the door, lying uncomfortably in bed, having taken something to bring on a fever to be used to explain his expired furlough pass. Finally the knocking came, rolling through the walls of the house. Madame Ackard opened the door for the armed men, and Willy could clearly hear their voices as they billowed up the attic stairs.

"Are there any young men in this house?!" they demanded.

"No," the small lady responded. A lie that, if found out, would heve ensured death.

"And, who is this?" they pointed to a framed photograph of someone in military uniform.

"My husband. Your prisoner," she responded flatly.

"And upstairs?"

"No one. Just an attic."

Through the back window, Willy saw the men searching around the house, even crawling through the chicken coop. Noting their thorough search, he considered his extraordinary good fortune. Firstly, that Ackard cared enough to lie for him, even while risking her own life. And secondly, that the soldiers had believed her enough to ignore the attic. Angels and good fortune.

The next morning my father got up and went to the window as

he did every morning. But this day, as he looked across the street toward the Del Hase market, he saw a long line of German military men as he'd never seen them before. They were disillusioned and depressed, heads hung low as they retreated through the town. Some pushed small children's wagons filled with meager belongings, as had their prisoners just a few years before. The higher-level SS would ride beside them in cars and on motorcycles. Back and forth and around them like shepherd dogs moving their herd, barking as they went.

"Look how you look," they yelled, "move faster, you pathetic *schweine*, what's the matter with you?! Have you no pride?!"

Willy couldn't believe the rush of emotion he felt on seeing this exodus. He climbed to the roof of the small house where he was able to see for miles. There were thousands of them, an endless line as far as the eye could see. They seemed to be followed from above by two American P–38 fighter planes. Each, with its double tail, seemed to taunt the men as it flew overhead, spraying them with machine gun fire, and dropping the occasional bomb. The German soldiers would run to the sides of the road as Willy had done just two years before. Once things seemed calm again, the Germans would recommence their retreat. And once again, the low-flying planes would appear with bullets and bombs. Watching this endless ritual all day long gave my father the strangest pleasure he could imagine. And though the victory was certainly an empty one, he suddenly felt no longer alone, but protected.

After some time, he saw the very men the soldiers had sought the evening before. Doors flew open all over town, and young gun-carrying Resistance fighters did exactly as the Germans had feared — what they had been doing in small villages throughout the retreat. They came out of hiding, shooting wildly at the retreating Nazi soldiers, making their flight that much more difficult. It was unclear to Willy whether they were trying to kill the retreating soldiers, or to simply impede the exodus and augment the Allies' ability to capture them. Perhaps it was unclear to the Resistance boys themselves, as nerves had certainly been rubbed raw. Regardless, they were extremely aggressive in their attacks, but knew enough to duck for cover whenever the occasional German tank would appear. Word had traveled that these "retreating" tanks had leveled entire villages as they rolled through, protecting their soldiers from vengeful townspeople. Provoking these German tanks was therefore obviously out of the question, so the "play" that unfolded on the small main street began to have a comical feel to it.

The town's citizens would throw open their doors and symbolically put up Belgian flags as the disheartened soldiers passed by, and the Resistance fighters would appear as if out of nowhere, shooting wholeheartedly. But then the rumbling of nearby tanks would announce their imminent arrival, and the civilians would quickly pull down the flags and hide behind their closed doors as the Resistance boys disappeared even faster than they'd appeared. The routine repeated itself over and over all day long.

Chapter Twenty

Tanks and Rainbows —
Willy and Mirele

The Liberation of Belgium, 1944

By the next morning, a Friday, the German tanks seemed to have finally vanished completely, along with the soldiers. Willy and Mirele were outside on the main road when they suddenly heard the heralding sound of more tanks approaching the village. But instead of clearing the streets to safety, they both found themselves riveted by a most extraordinary sight — a giant rainbow rose in a perfect and beautiful arch above the main road into town, more vibrant and luminous than anything either of them had ever seen. And then, driving right through it, as if it were a magical portal, was their liberator. As the huge metal beast rolled through, my parents could clearly see the large white star that distinguished it from that of their enemy.... And so it was, that directly through this awesome, magical rainbow, came the first American tank.

Suddenly, the tank's hatch was thrown open by a young American major, still in helmet. A dozen local girls clamored up the sides of the tank to get to him; my father couldn't help but smile when he realized Mirele was the first up.

"But of course she would be," he thought to himself. "There was no one quite like her."

Then, in a scene that could have found its way to a cover of *Life* magazine, all these euphoric young girls began to grab and kiss the officer. All but one — my mother — who simply wept.

"Why are you crying?" the officer asked, noticing the difference in her greeting.

"They're tears of joy," she told him in her perfect English. "You see, I am a Jew" — words she uttered freely for the first time since her early teens. "And I am so very happy to see you."

"Well," he answered directly to her, despite all the other young women who clamored, now unnoticed, about him, "I'm a Jew too." And he embraced her tightly, letting her tears flow.

It was Friday, and that evening would be the first Shabbat for my parents as free Jews since the war began. So, there atop the American tank, Mirele invited the major to join her family for the Sabbath dinner.

"It would be my honor," he replied.

He came to dinner at the Linchamps's house that evening accompanied by a young soldier. The dinner was an extraordinary mix of emotions. My mother's emotions overtook her once again, and she began to cry.

"Oh, look, she's in love with the first American she sees," Madame Linchamps teased lovingly in French so the soldiers wouldn't understand.

"That's not why I'm crying at all," Mirele answered through the tears. "I'm crying because we were liberated by a Jew. This man, the major. And because, you see, we are all Jews too."

When the shock passed, Madame Linchamps began to cry right along with my mother that night. And then, in a strange turn of events, she was joined by her husband.

"We didn't know what Jews are," he said, perhaps remembering some of the strange conversations of the weeks before. "We are so very sorry. We understand everything now."

Because Brussels had also just been liberated, Willy, Mirele, and her parents decided to return there immediately. Willy went back to Helen's where he found his brother still in residence, and

200

Mirele and her parents to the apartment at 16 Rues des Echelles, to the delight of the generous *Bomma* Abrams.

The streets were in chaos. Liberation was much more than a military victory. It was an emotion, a state of being... a way of life. The city was one huge week-long party. American tanks were everywhere, as were jeeps and trucks. There was still a military presence, to be certain, but instead of the oppressive Germans, there were Americans and British boys, all delighted with their heroes' welcome. The happiness was intoxicating. No one seemed capable of doing much of anything besides celebrating... and so celebrate they did.

The moment he returned, Willy took to the streets with his 10,000 "Liberté" brooches. He presented the first box of one hundred to the crowd, and sold them almost before he could display them. He took the remaining pins to a dealer who purchased the balance of the ten thousand for cash on the spot, and later reported he had sold them all that very day.

Benny showed up within days to take my mother and Willy out into the nightlife. They met up with some of his newest American military friends and danced the night away. Though my mother had been a good dancer in her teens, even having won a tango contest during the youth club days, the war had left little opportunity for dancing. So, when a young American soldier pulled her to the floor and began to jitterbug, the new dance was totally unfamiliar and the results of her attempt had her roaring with laughter.

Now, though Brussels was liberated, the Allies were short on reinforcements and faced the problem of maintaining fuel and supply lines. So, even with the German army retreating, the Allies were not yet able to push forward across the Rhine into Germany itself. Hitler had been on the defensive for a while now, but the best of his SS guards, his personal divisions, suddenly turned things back around. Specific officers, chosen for their perfect English, came into Belgium wearing American uniforms, and strategically changed all the directional signs throughout the countryside routing all the Allied troops to a town called Bastogne. They then made an offensive entrance back into the country, directly to Bastogne, where they encircled all the Americans they had routed there. The Germans took about one hundred American prisoners that day, but lacked sufficient means of holding them. So, just as the Germans had already done with so many of their concentration camp civilian prisoners, on December 17, 1944, in Malmédy, France, the Nazis massacred these young American soldiers.

The haze had been so thick that day that the Americans were unable to fight back with the planes that had become their strength. During the battle, the German commander sent word to the American General McAuliffe, demanding his surrender.

The general advised the courier to return to his commander and tell him simply, "Nuts."

Word of Germany's seeming success quickly made its way to Brussels, and Willy knew if they continued to succeed, Belgium would once again be in German hands. He told Mirele and her parents to ready themselves for travel, and decided that if the Germans made it to the River Maas, they would have both reason and time to run. Fortunately, that day never came.

Within days, history was made as General Patton moved his troops in to free the remaining American prisoners, in what would later be immortalized as the "Battle of the Bulge." These battles of the Ardennes would be remembered as some of the most brutal of the war, and with the greatest number of military casualties. Cloudy weather prevented the full use of air power, but after three weeks, the haze was replaced with sunshine. And with the sun, came American planes that had been awaiting this very opportunity. They dropped food and munitions for their soldiers, and bombed the Germans where possible. First pushing the Germans back and breaking their strategic encirclement of the Allies; then pushing them further back yet, all the way into Germany. The encirclement of the Americans at Bastogne during those first foggy days would be the last German stand of the war. From that moment on, the Germans would experience nothing but defeat.

Liberation was now real. Willy and Benny worked for the OSS, the CIA's predecessor, for a short time. They were stationed in Compiègne, France, where they would spend their days as civilians, listening to gossip and chatting with strangers. Their job was to find the names of locals who had been Nazi sympathizers during the occupation. With his flare for the dramatic, Benny took the job rather seriously, sporting two Dragnet-style gun holsters across his chest.

My father had started his life over from nothing so many times, that his current plight didn't seem to daunt him. Getting cash was simply a matter of time. He visited Benny's friend, Warren, whose mother was once again housing his in-laws, at the back of a small café that was the new makeshift diamond exchange in Brussels.

"I'm an artist with a good eye," Willy began his proposition. "I know diamonds and can make you money. Give me a little cash, let me work for you, buying and selling. Then we'll split the profits."

Warren, always up for a gamble, gave Willy the money. He bought several diamonds and knew he only had seven hours to sell them before the doors were to close. By the end of the day, he had sold the diamonds and returned with sufficient profit to encourage the partnership into the weeks that followed.

While he continued trading in diamonds with Warren, he

persuaded Mirele to look for work with the British military. He recommended she try at the local Palace Hotel, where the British had set up military headquarters.

"What could I do there?" Mirele questioned helplessly.

"Tell them you're a secretary."

"But I've no skills."

"Then be an interpreter. They must need them, and you speak so many languages perfectly."

This conversation continued for a week; she spoke of her liabilities, and Willy of her assets, until finally, she agreed. Applying for the job was much easier than she anticipated. The soldiers who had set up shop in the rather grand Palace Hotel on Boulevard Botanique were as friendly as could be. She was now a very tough twenty-one, who, despite her last years of emotional hardships, had somehow held on to her enormous love of laughter. Her eyes still managed to twinkle and her smile, outlined in bright red French lipstick, opened all the right doors.

"Of course we need interpreters," the young sergeant smiled right back at her. "As a matter of fact, I think Captain Thiem has been looking for a secretary that can help him with French, German and Flemish... You do speak all three, right?"

"Yes, but my secretarial skills...," she began, but was quickly cut off.

"Don't worry. The languages are the hard part and your English is great. I'll help you with the typing."

My mother began working the very next day. And before she knew it, she was one of the only employees welcomed in every office. Her relationship with the sergeant grew, as she leaned on him to keep his word about helping her out. She would be called in for dictation, and because of the captain's speed in delivery, and her lack of skill, she'd leave his office and head straight to the young soldier.

204

"He did it again. He went so quickly, I've only the first letter of each word this time."

"Who was it to?" the young man asked.

"Here. See if you can figure it out."

And so began their common exercise of deciphering and transcribing her "notes." Everyone in the office took a liking to the young Belgian girl, and before she knew it, favors began to flow.

One day the restaurant's official knife-sharpener approached the captain: "Sir, my grandmother has some German marks... from before the war. I'm afraid they're rather worthless now... would there be any way you might help me in exchanging them for dollars?"

"I think that can be managed," the captain offered.

When the knife-sharpener left, Mirele couldn't help but comment, wanting to educate her generous boss, "You know, Captain, those marks weren't his old grandmother's."

"I know," he responded with a small smile, "but I'm sure exchanging them might give him a bit of a hand, don't you think? These are difficult times." Then, after a beat, "Mirele, does your old grandmother happen to have any marks she might need exchanged?"

First surprised, but quick on the uptake, Mirele replied, "I do believe she does, Sir."

When she returned home that evening she told Willy of the offer and he immediately went out onto the streets to buy as many German marks as he could find and afford on the black market. She brought them to the captain, and was delighted to find an envelope filled with dollars on her desk the following morning — profiting probably tenfold.

One day at the diamond exchange, Willy made the acquaintance of two brothers who were also photographers.

"We should be doing what we're skilled to do," they pressed him, when they heard that he was one too. "Let's become partners."

"And what?" Willy said. "I've only one small camera. I lost everything."

"We have everything we need. We even already have an automatic photo machine down the block."

Together, the three opened another photo booth. Business was so good, they soon had four more on the three main streets in Brussels. The streets were teeming with American and British soldiers, who all wanted souvenirs of their part in world history, or sometimes of their romance. Each small storefront was constantly blessed with an excited line of customers ready to pay for their keepsake.

In addition, the enterprising trio rented a porch and several stores where they began selling cameras. Each also had a portrait studio somewhere inside it. The film from all the photographers would make its way to Willy, who would work all night developing and retouching all the portraits.

Though the business was proving successful, my father missed the privacy of his own studio. He explained to his partners he needed to open his own place too, and asked Mirele if there was anyone that could help them secure an apartment. The next day she approached the British major who frequented the restaurant at the Palace Hotel, and whose main responsibility was the de-requisition of Brussels properties that had been taken over by the Nazis during the occupation.

"Excuse me, Major," Mirele asked nervously, "I was wondering if you could help my family and me rent an apartment here in Brussels. It's really quite impossible to get one with the military taking over and all... and we've lost everything, you know."

"I'm sure I can... just give me a couple of days," he responded kindly, when he heard she and her parents had been out of their home for years, and had been living in cramped quarters with their elderly friend. Using his position to right things, he was able to de-requisition two empty floors above a nearby shoe store for my father, my mother, and grandparents to occupy.

Willy worked out the specifics of rent and so forth with the landlord, and the extended family moved in. Though keeping up his participation in the other enterprises, Willy soon reopened the doors to "Studio Willy" on the ground floor. In addition, he helped Mirele and her mother open a lingerie boutique on the second floor, and hired a man to parade out front in a sandwich board that advertised: "Lingerie en haute."

Much of the world's silk having been requisitioned for parachutes, silk stockings were replaced with nylons, and my mother and grandmother did very well marketing them to the young soldiers along with "French" underwear of all kinds. Souria, my grandmother, had only a small grasp of English and would repeat her one sales pitch over and over again.

"Shining and lining together," she would say with great sensuous enthusiasm as she ran her hand over her delicate wares, displaying them to her clientele. More often than not, the young soldiers would smile and purchase her goods. So, having deduced that the sales pitch worked, she emphasized it even more the next time.

As his assets grew, Willy soon opened a camera store, but inventory was hard to come by. Willing to purchase anything second-hand, he sent a buyer to the nearby hotels to approach the foreign military men for their cameras. In no time at all, everyone in Belgium came to his shop, as it was the only store in the country with an inventory. And as his own inventory grew, he soon began to supply all the other stores as well.

Money now flowing, he purchased a beautiful Rosenthal tea set as a gift for my mother. She was so delighted with the fine china that she soon invited her kind boss over to tea. When Willy saw her serving Captain Thiem with "his" tea set, he felt something begin to stir inside him. By the time the captain left the apartment, the stirring had risen into a wave of anger that found Willy violently throwing the fine china to the ground. As he watched it crash into a thousand pieces, the wave rose into a full-blown typhoon, and he broke into the captain's office, threateningly holding a gun on the officer's desk.

"Stay away from my sister-in-law," my father demanded. "She's a married woman."

The captain most certainly could have had Willy arrested, but chose to do nothing, motivated perhaps by fear, but more likely by compassion for what the quick-tempered young survivor had been through. Willy left the building a strange jumble of emotions, and most probably with no clear idea of what those emotions tearing through him really were.

In May 1945, the war was finally over, and the camp survivors began to return home. Frustrated, with little knowledge of her young husband's fate, Mirele was thrilled to hear from someone who had recently seen him.

"Izi's alive. He's left Buchenwald... they've taken him to Theresienstadt," she was told by one man.

Theresienstadt, once a camp just outside Prague, was now a hospital. Izi had apparently survived two camps and then, finally, the death march that culminated at Buchenwald. When the liberators realized he'd contracted typhus, he was moved to the makeshift hospital.

"He wanted to recuperate for a few more days before coming home to his young wife," the man explained. "He didn't want you to see him looking the way he was."

Three more survivors came into Willy's studio at different times, all giving the same report of Izi's situation. Mirele had confided much of her story to a rather kind major who frequented the military offices at the Palace Hotel. Major Joseph, an English Jew and heir to the Lyons Tea fortune, was in charge of the Catering Corps for the entire British military installation in Europe. He would frequently pass through Brussels on official business. When doing so, he became well-acquainted with the young secretary, even using her dictation services on occasion.

"Any news on your husband?" he asked Mirele during one such visit.

Mirele couldn't hold her emotions any longer and burst into tears. "He hasn't been sent home. Some say they think he has contracted typhus...."

"Do you know his location?"

"Yes... I think he's in Theresienstadt being treated," she responded.

"I'm leaving for Czechoslovakia in the morning. Prepare a valise and I'll personally escort you by jeep. We'll bring him home."

Delighted, my mother quickly ran home and did exactly as he'd ordered. But as she packed her small bag, Benny came in to stop her journey.

"I've just been to Place Rouppe. I met a man there who said Izi saved his life. Carried him on his shoulders the entire death march.... Amazing man, your husband! I told him you were about to leave to fetch him and he insisted it was a mistake. He says Izi's probably on his way back right now."

Place Rouppe was a square that had become known as a meeting place for those returning from the camps. It was the place where everyone went to reconnect with missing loved ones —

209

family or friends. If they couldn't be found there, news of their status usually could. Some people even wore signs with names and/or pictures of those whom they were searching for, hoping that might elicit information from strangers who had possibly seen them.

With Benny's warning that she might cross Izi's path on the way to find him, Mirele cancelled the trip and waited impatiently for his return. Her mind was without rest... she thought about how much she'd changed, and wondered about him constantly. But the days quickly turned into weeks without his arrival.

By this time, things were starting to change at the Palace Hotel. First, there had been a command rotation, with Captain Thiem being replaced by Captain Hill, a tough military man now badly crippled with arthritis. Secondly, when the Russian allies needed to set up an embassy in Brussels, the British offered them the twelfth floor of the hotel. Though they were allies, relations were strangely strained, so on the day of the Russians' official and rather pompous arrival, Captain Hill decided to show them the least hospitality possible. Quite aware that protocol mandated that a representative greet them, and with no intention of doing so himself, Hill opted to send his young right hand.

"Welcome our fellow liberators," he ordered young Mirele.

She stood beside him, looking through the window at the official Russian motorcade that had just pulled up in front of the Palace Hotel, and at the stern men pouring out onto the sidewalk in their fur hats and heavy epaulet-bearing, gold-and fur-trimmed coats.

Taking a rather deep breath, my mother did exactly as she'd been told and introduced herself, with a grand welcome and heartfelt enormous thanks for Russian help in her personal

210

liberation. She immediately added that her parents were immigrants from Odessa. The Russian official in charge took one look at my mother's high cheekbones, and pinched them lovingly.

"You no Belgie...," he said with a robust chuckle and very broken French, "you Ruskie."

From that day onward, she was as good as one of them. The Russians soon posted guards at every entrance to their floor, sealing it off completely. No one from the British floors was allowed to enter — no one... except the young secretary. In fact, Mirele had somehow managed to be the only person who could roam freely throughout the entire hotel. No office was off-limits. Furthermore, if the Brits wanted vodka or caviar, she was sent up to fetch it. If the Russians had a need the British could supply, a well-aged Scotch, perhaps, she was sent down. And all the while, her outgoing personality and gift of gab made her story well known.

With the Russians liberating Czechoslovakia, things there became more complicated, including travel. So when the weeks had passed with no sight of Izi, she made her way up to the top floor, telling the Russian commander of her plight. He immediately penned a letter of introduction for her, advising that any person she came across should do whatever they could to aid her search for her husband.

"With this, you will have no problems," he said, handing her the letter.

"Thank you so much," she said with sincere gratitude, taking the official documents from his hand.

She collected her things as soon as she could and ran to see my father at his shop.

"I'm leaving to find Izi. I've got Russian papers in my purse. An official at the embassy has arranged everything," she told

Willy with nervous enthusiasm. "I'm so scared. I've never even been out of the country."

Willy looked at her hard. He'd been spending so much time with her lately, he never really thought about what things would be like when Izi returned. She looked so beautiful and alive. So mature. No longer the baby sister of his wife, but an extraordinary woman who'd made it through the war strangely unscathed. And she had even helped him through some rather difficult times.

"Get your things," was all he could think of saying. "I'll take you to the station."

Before he knew it, she was back in the store, a small bag in hand. He grabbed his overcoat off a nearby rack, and slid into it while reaching for his hat. He looked hard at Mirele again as he placed his hat comfortably onto his head, slightly tilted to the side.

"Everything will be fine," he said, as he gently passed his arm through hers and guided her out of the shop. Somehow the anger he'd felt toward the captain was beginning to make sense.

"You'll see. Everything will be fine."

On the way to the station Willy wondered about the stories they'd heard about Izi's health. He felt a strange ache in his stomach as he realized Izi was more likely dead than alive. It was painful to think about how difficult this journey would be for Mirele. He felt a peculiar swirl of emotions... and of loneliness. Maybe his. Maybe hers. He wondered who could ever deal with the ghosts that lived in his heart, and then suddenly he knew, and he felt almost guilty for the attraction that accompanied these emotions and realizations.

Why is it when we race through a crowd we hear only our footsteps? Frantic, clicking. The only thing that will possibly drown them out is the sound of our own heartbeat as it pounds in our ears. My father seemed as anxious as my mother to get to the train. When they finally arrived and he helped her on, he didn't say good-bye.

"If you get to Theresienstadt, and Izi is dead, I want you to marry me."

Not your usual proposal. Not your usual romance. But it was theirs.

As the train pulled away he wondered about his words. He didn't mean to be so cold, but the war had made that which had once been unthinkable, common facts of everyday life. His head reeled as he stood there watching Mirele's train until it had traveled out of sight. He stood there for what seemed an eternity thinking about the past....

...And then, finally, wondering about the future.

Epilogue

My mother took the difficult train ride to find out the fate of her husband; her childhood sweetheart; her Izi. The ride was long, and the train was crowded and cold. The car she rode in was not a normal passenger wagon, but some type of altered cargo car. There were seats helter-skelter, and a fire burned in the center of the car to keep the freezing passengers warm as they traveled through Eastern Europe. It was a strange trip to have been her first.

A Czech doctor who rode with her helped make the time pass quickly. He had a calming effect and proved to be a welcome companion. Though he was married, she realized there was certainly flirtation on his part, and with that came the additional realization that she was no longer a teen, but a woman. By the time the train reached its destination, he had given her addresses of people and places where she might find help, and perhaps a tiny bit more confidence than that with which she had started the ride. Disembarking was therefore much easier than it might have been without the good fortune of the meeting.

She went directly to a Red Cross station... and it was a very short time after arriving in this foreign and chaotic city, that she found Izi's name on a list of recently deceased. The cause of death was listed as typhus, but in reality this disease, which he may have contracted, was far from the cause of the young man's death.

Izi died six weeks after liberation... one of the millions of innocent victims of the Nazi concentration and death camps.

Mirele spent the night in a small pension room whose appearance went totally unnoticed by her. She wasn't even sure what she felt that night. To the world, Izi's premature death would become nothing more than a well-known statistic, but to Mirele, it was a love lost and never to be forgotten. But there had been so many losses... so much pain. She wasn't certain if she had ever really believed she would find her husband alive... or that they would have even recognized each other if she did. They both had gone through so very much these last years. Emotions ran through her as quickly and confusingly as her thoughts did. And if sleep ever came, it was only through exhaustion.

Returning to Brussels, Mirele would recognize the love that had grown for Willy deep inside her heart, and she would eventually take my father up on his proposal of marriage. The years in hiding had brought them closer than lifetimes might have brought other couples. Together they did not share the innocence of first love, for that had been stolen from them by the Nazis. But instead, my parents shared the depth of a love that grew through the most profound sense of history, of loss, of understanding... and maybe most of all, of a passion for survival.

> "It is good to have an end to journey toward.
> But it is the journey that matters in the end."
> Ursula K. LeGuin

Acknowledgments

p. 5

Frankl,Viktor E., *Man's Search for Meaning.* Copyright © 1959, 1962, 1984, 1992 by Viktor Frankl. Reprinted by permission of Beacon Press, Boston, Mass. 2000. Additional permission by the Viktor E. Frankl Institute, Vienna, Austria.

p. 19

Huffington, Arianna, *The Gods of Greece.* Reprinted by permission of Arianna Huffington. Internet, 2001.

p. 101

Fowles, John, *The Magus.* Revised Edition Copyright © 1977 by John Fowles. First Edition Copyright © 1965 by John Fowles. Reprinted by permission of the author. A Laurel Book, Dell Publishing, New York. NY. 1965.

p. 109

Al Hanisim prayer. Didactic adaptation by Chaim Weinreb. Reprinted by permission of Department for Jewish Zionist Education, JAFI. Internet.

p. 216

LeGuin, Ursula K., Unknown source. Reprinted by permission of the author.

For permission to use copyrighted material, we thank the above literary executors and publishers. We have made every effort to obtain permission to reprint material in this book and to publish proper acknowledgments, and regret any error or oversight.